The Modern Age

Peter & Mary Speed

Oxford University Press by arrangement with the British Broadcasting Corporation

© Peter and Mary Speed 1980

First published 1980
Reprinted 1981 (twice)

Oxford University Press, Walton Street, Oxford OX2 6DP

ISBN 0 19 918122 5

London   Glasgow   New York   Toronto
Delhi   Bombay   Calcutta   Madras   Karachi
Kuala Lumpur   Singapore   Hong Kong   Tokyo
Nairobi   Dar es Salaam   Cape Town   Salisbury
Melbourne   Auckland

and associate companies in
Beirut   Berlin   Ibadan   Mexico City

Typesetting by Tradespools Ltd., Frome, Somerset
Printed in Hong Kong

Contents

Chapter One   Transport and Exploration

1 Ocean Liners

1897 was the year of Queen Victoria's Diamond Jubilee. There was a grand review of the fleet at Spithead. One hundred and sixty-five battleships were drawn up in three lines, each thirty miles long. The Prince of Wales took the salute, sailing near the battleships in the royal yacht. Suddenly, a small boat appeared and began dashing in and out among the lines of ships. Fast Admiralty launches at once chased after her, but the small boat shot through the water at nearly 35 knots (40 m.p.h.) and the launches could not go nearly as fast. The boat was called the *Turbinia*, and belonged to Sir Charles Parsons. He had invented a new type of engine and he was determined that everyone should see how good it was. This engine was a steam turbine. It was much simpler

than an ordinary steam engine, but it was also much more powerful.

The *Turbinia* certainly attracted a lot of attention. It was not long before shipbuilders were using turbines in much larger vessels. Then the Cunard Company became interested. The ship that crossed the Atlantic in the shortest time was awarded a prize called the 'Blue Riband'. At that time the Germans held the record but the Cunard Company was planning to build two gigantic liners, the *Mauretania* and the *Lusitania*. Perhaps Parsons's turbines would help Cunard win the Blue Riband for Great Britain? No one knew how turbines would work in a vessel weighing 31,000 tons, but Cunard was willing to try. The *Mauretania* made her maiden voyage in November

the *Turbina*

1907. It was a terrible crossing, but she won the Blue Riband for Great Britain. The liner was in service for twenty-eight years, and she held the Blue Riband for twenty-two of them.

We will pay the *Mauretania* a visit, and one of her stewards will show us round.

'You will see the *Mauretania* has four funnels,' he says. 'That's very important to the passengers. They think it means a ship is among the best afloat. Some liners even have a dummy funnel to make up the four because some passengers won't sail on a ship that has fewer than four funnels.'

The ship has seven decks. We go from one to the other in an electric lift. Some people think of a liner as a floating hotel but the *Mauretania* is more like a floating town! There are many cabins, of course, as well as various public rooms: a library, a writing room, a drawing room, a lounge, a smoking room and a grand saloon for meals and entertainment. There are so many flowers and plants that gardeners are needed to look after them.

'One of our main problems is to stop the passengers becoming bored,' continues the steward. 'There are all sorts of games they can play, like shuffleboard and deck tennis. In the evening there is dancing, or sometimes a show. I dread the shows. The passengers take part themselves, you see. Some of them think they can sing or dance or tell funny stories, but usually they can't and it's embarrassing to watch. When there is nothing else to do, they can go for a walk. Four times round the promenade deck is a mile. Some people who never go for a walk on land do so at sea. One man covered a hundred miles between Liverpool and

the promenade deck of the *Lusitania*

New York. The passengers get most excited at noon, when our captain says how many miles we have sailed in the day. They lay bets on it, you see.'

'*How far do you usually sail in one day?*' 'Over six hundred miles – quite often.' '*Do the passengers enjoy their voyage?*' 'Not as much as they think they will. We spend five days at sea, and most passengers spend the

the first-class lounge of the *Lusitania*

Ocean Liners

a cross-section of the *Mauretania*

first two days being sick. For the next three they still have to put up with the pitch and roll of the ship. The first-class passengers are amidships, so it's not too bad for them. The third-class passengers are at the front where it is nothing for them to rise and fall fifty feet in rough seas.'

'*How do you enjoy life at sea?*' we ask the steward. 'I have to put up with silly questions from passengers. They ask the same ones every voyage – Do you carry any sails in case the engines break down? How does the captain know the way? How

do the brakes work on a ship like this? Still, many of them tip quite well, so I don't complain. If you want to know what it's like for some of the crew though, come and see the "Black Gang".'

The steward leads us to the boiler room where the stokers are at work. The noise, heat and smell are overpowering. A stoker opens a furnace door and rakes out a shower of red-hot ashes. He then spreads four or five shovels of coal over the fire and shuts the furnace door with a clang. He is caked with dust and sweat.

'He has to do that every seven minutes,' says the steward. 'You can imagine what it's like in a gale. These men are really hard. I have seen that one brought on board in a wheelbarrow, dead drunk. There are dreadful fights, too. Usually it's when they are on land, but we have had fights at sea. The only thing to do then is to slam down the hatches and let them get on with it. I heard of an officer on another ship who interfered in a fight and was never seen again. They split open his head with a shovel, and then flung him into the furnace.'

1 bridge **2** wheel house **3** captain's cabin **4** officers' accommodation **5** ventilators **6** cargo hoists **7** engine room **8** turbines **9** boilers **10** control platform **11** wireless room **12** 'A' or boat deck **13** 'B' or promenade deck **14** 'upper C' or shelter deck **15** 'C' or upper deck **16** 'D' or main deck **17** 'E' or lower deck **18** 1st class lounge **19** 1st class smoke room **20** 1st class dining saloon **21** 1st class staircase and lifts **22** 1st class library **23** 1st class accommodation **24** musicians' gallery **25** 2nd class lounge **26** 2nd class drawing room **27** 2nd class dining saloon **28** 2nd class accommodation **29** 3rd class dining saloon **30** 3rd class public rooms **31** 3rd class accommodation **32** nursery **33** hospital **34** bank **35** bathrooms **36** engine room hatches **37** regal suite **38** printing offices

2 The First Motor Cars

Who invented the motor car? It is really impossible to say, for many people had a hand in it. It all began thousands of years ago when someone invented the wheel. Much later, people learnt how to make light, fast carriages with proper axles, springs and comfortable seats. By the early nineteenth century there were carriages driven by steam engines. Some worked quite well, but were unpopular and soon went out of use.

There was a big step forward in about 1860 when a Frenchman called Lenoir invented a gas engine. His engines provided power for factories and workshops. People were glad to have them because they were so easy to start and stop. There was no need to light a fire and wait for water to boil as with steam engines. Lenoir also used his engines to drive carriages but they did not work very well.

At about the same time, companies were beginning to drill for oil. From the crude oil they made lubricating oil, and paraffin for lighting. They found that the liquid they were left with burst into flames very easily. They thought it was too dangerous to use,

an 1898 Benz

so they threw it away. It was called 'benzine'. We know it as petrol.

Then someone said, 'Benzine turns into a gas very easily, so why not use it in an engine like Lenoir's?' Several people tried to make petrol engines. In the 1880s two Germans, Gottlieb Daimler and Karl Benz succeeded. They started firms which are still making motor cars today. Other Germans copied them. The French were not far behind.

What was happening in Britain? Here Parliament had made a law for the big steam tractor engines used on farms. It said that each one must have three men to drive it, that it must not go over three m.p.h. and that someone must walk in front of it to give warning, usually with a red flag. No one had dreamt of motor cars when this law had been made. But people who bought French or German cars found they were expected to obey it. In 1896 Parliament at last changed the law and made motoring legal. The few people who owned cars celebrated by driving from London to Brighton.

We will now visit the village of Midsomer Norton, ten miles from Bath. It is 1906 and we go to see the local doctor, Dr. Bulleid. He is the only man in the village to own a car. It is a Panhard, made in France. It has black shining bodywork, a polished brass radiator and lamps, and seats of red leather.

'*Why did you buy this car, Doctor?*' 'It's convenient for visiting my patients, but I still keep my horse and carriage because the car is quite likely to break down. Mainly, I like it for amusement during my spare time. If it's fine this afternoon I will go out on the Bath road.' '*You mean you will go to Bath?*' 'I mean I will go in that direction,' laughs the doctor. 'If I arrive, it will be a pleasant surprise.' '*What can go wrong?*' 'A puncture is the most likely thing. I once punctured all four of my tyres in ten miles. Our roads were made for carts, not motor cars. I hear that in some places they have a new kind of road surface called tarmacadam. I hope we will have it on our roads soon. The engine often goes wrong, of course. I have learnt a lot about car engines by putting this one right and helping other motorists. If we see someone in trouble on the road we always stop and try to help.'

'*What do the local people think of your car?*' 'Most

Dr. Bulleid and his new Panhard

the London to Brighton race today

of them just come out of their houses and gape when I drive by. They are amazed to see a horseless carriage. Farmers don't like cars, because they frighten their horses. I startled a milkman's horse the other day. The animal bolted and there were upset churns and milk all over the road. The police are a nuisance; they are always setting speed-traps. They hide behind hedges with stop-watches. The A.A. Scouts are a great help in spotting speed-traps. They used to wave a red disc or salute as a warning, but the magistrates said this was against the law. Now, the Scouts only salute when the road is clear and are careful *not* to salute if there is a police trap. A man can hardly be fined for doing nothing, can he?'

'*Have you had any accidents, Doctor?*' 'The car ran away once when I parked on a steep hill. The brakes are not very good, you see, so now when I stop on a hill, the first thing I do is put a brick behind one of the wheels. My coachman hurt himself and the car rather badly a few weeks ago. He is more used to horses than to motor cars. He came up the drive rather fast and forgot to brake or turn off the engine. We heard him crash through the garage doors shouting, "Whoa, you devil, whoa!" '

9

3 The Austin Seven

In the early 1920s a new car appeared in the show-rooms – the Austin Seven. We will visit a family who have just bought one. *'Are you pleased with your new car, Mr. Brown?'* 'Delighted!' *'It's not very big, is it?'* 'It's just right for us. My wife and I sit in the front. We lift the two children over the seats and put them in the back where they are out of harm's way. I know a farmer who drives his fat wife to market in his Austin Seven, and he takes two large friends as well. The engine just about copes, but the body of his car is beginning to crack. It's his own fault. He puts too much strain on his car.'

'How fast does she go?' 'Once we went over fifty miles an hour, but it frightened my wife so I haven't tried that again. The car nips up hills easily. Richer motorists laugh at the Austin Seven and call it a "bath tub on wheels" or a "motorized pram", but we often overtake bigger cars. We wave at them as we go past! If you have paid £500 for a car it upsets you to be passed by one that only costs £165!'

'Do you have any trouble with it?' 'Well, I have to watch the oil pressure. I keep an eye on that little knob. If it sticks out I have to stop the car, take out four little plugs and poke some holes clean with a bit of wire. It doesn't take long, and hasn't happened often. No, we can rely on our Austin Seven to take us anywhere.'

'What do you think of the car, Mrs. Brown?' 'I can't tell you how pleased I am. My husband used to talk about buying a motor bike and sidecar, but you would never get me on a pillion in all winds and weathers. I wouldn't like the children cooped up together in a sidecar, either. They would certainly be uncomfortable and they wouldn't be able to talk to us. We often looked longingly at the cars in the show-rooms but we never thought we'd be able to afford one. Now, we can go out every weekend, either into the country or to the seaside. We are going on holiday in it this summer. Think how much easier it will be than on the train!'

'It's good for my work, too,' adds Mr. Brown. 'I don't have to cycle or catch the bus, so I am home much earlier than before. In fact, we are thinking of buying a new house, right out of the town. It will be much nicer for the family, and I will be able to drive to my office quite easily.'

'*Do you drive, Mrs. Brown?*' 'I tried once, but after what my husband said to me, never again!' 'She had trouble with the clutch!' explains Mr. Brown. 'She just couldn't let the clutch pedal out smoothly enough. She made the car jump like a kangaroo. Goodness knows what damage she did. She nearly shook the children out of the back seat.'

Now we will visit Mr. Tupton, who helps to make Austin Sevens. '*Where do you work, Mr. Tupton?*' 'At Longbridge, near Birmingham. It is hard to believe there was only a derelict factory there less than twenty years ago. I joined the firm when Sir Herbert Austin started it. We only made Austin Twenties then. Beautiful cars they are, but expensive. During the Great War we had to go over to making munitions. Of course, the plant covered acres of ground by then. There were over 20,000 of us working there at one time. Soon after the War ended, when the big cars didn't sell any more, it looked as if we were going to lose our jobs. Then Sir Herbert had this bright idea

one of the first Austin Sevens

later version of the Austin Seven

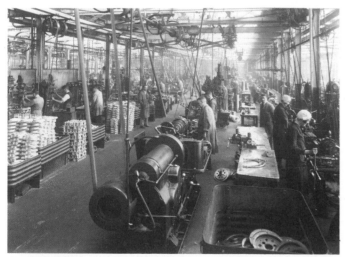
the Austin Seven production line

of making a cheap, little car that ordinary folk could buy. Everyone laughs at the Austin Sevens, but they sell like hot cakes!'

But Austin Sevens could do more than take a family out for a weekend drive. In August 1978, holiday makers on the roads of Scotland were surprised to see convoys of Austin Sevens, many still in good condition, heading towards the town of Fort William. About eighty of the old cars were making their way to a special rally in the town, which is at the foot of Ben Nevis, the highest mountain in Great Britain. Fifty years before, a Mr. George Simpson drove to the top of Ben Nevis, in an Austin Seven fitted with a specially low first gear. The car reached the top in 7 hours, 23 minutes and came down again in 1 hour, 55 minutes, a time which still stands in the *Guinness Book of Records*. This was a great triumph for the little Austin. Even today, no other ordinary car has ever reached the top of Ben Nevis.

4 The First Aeroplanes

For thousands of years men watched birds soaring through the air and longed to do the same. The obvious way to fly seemed to be to make a pair of wings and flap them, but this idea never worked. No one is strong enough to carry his own weight into the air. There was another way to fly, though, and that was by balloon. Ballooning became quite a popular sport, but it is not really flying like birds. You can only go where the wind takes you.

During the nineteenth century, many inventors tried new ways of flying. One of them was Sir George Cayley, who showed that flapping wings would never be any use. A better idea was to have fixed wings and

the Lilienthal glider

drive the aircraft with a propellor. Several people built models that flew quite well, and others made gliders. A German called Otto Lilienthal managed to pilot a glider for three hundred yards. He made many flights but in 1896 his glider crashed into a hillside and he was killed.

A big problem was to find a suitable motor. At first, only steam engines were available, which were far too heavy. Then, in the 1880s Benz and Daimler developed the petrol engine. They had used it to drive a carriage. Would it be possible to make it drive a glider? Several people decided to try, including two American brothers, Wilbur and Orville Wright.

The Wright brothers were brought up in Dayton, Ohio. They were both very ingenious inventors. As young lads they made a printing press from scrap metal and an old tombstone. When they grew up they started a small business, mending and making bicycles. In 1896, the same year that Otto Lilienthal was killed, Orville Wright nearly died from typhoid fever, and as he was recovering he had plenty of time to think. He and Wilbur had been interested in flying for a long time. They decided they would try and make an aeroplane.

The two brothers went to work carefully. They realized that the first thing they had to do was to learn to glide. They left Dayton and went 400 miles away to Kittyhawk. This was a little village on a narrow sand bar, just off the coast of North Carolina. Here the wind blew steadily and there was a bare hill called Kill Devil Hill which was just right for launching a glider.

They built three gliders, each better than the last. Between them they made over 1,000 flights, and learnt how to control their craft in the air. Then, in 1903, they built another machine, this time with a motor and two propellors— the first aeroplane. On Kill Devil Hill they made a sloping track. Their aeroplane had skids, so that it would slide down the track like a toboggan, and gain enough speed to take off. By December 14th, 1903 everything was ready. The two brothers tossed a coin to decide who would try to fly first, and Wilbur won. He started the engine. The aeroplane raced down the track and began to rise. Almost at once its nose shot through the air. The

the Wright brothers' first flight

aeroplane stalled, dropped back to the ground and fell sideways. Luckily, Wilbur was not hurt and there was little damage to the machine. By December 17th they had repaired it and now it was Orville's turn to take the controls. Again the aeroplane shot down the track. Wilbur ran beside it for a few seconds, but then it rose gently and left him behind. Orville stayed in the air for twelve seconds and flew 120 feet. This was the first flight ever made in a powered, heavier-than-air machine.

Delighted with their success, the brothers at once made some more flights. On the last one Wilbur was in the air for 59 seconds and flew over 850 feet. He crash-landed in the sand, damaging the machine slightly. They carried it back to the hangar, but on the way a gust of wind turned it over and smashed it to pieces. So ended one of the most important days in the history of flight.

Wilbur and Orville Wright had worked almost entirely on their own among the sand dunes of Kittyhawk. Only a handful of friends came to see their first flight. Hardly any newspapers reported it and few of the people who did hear of it believed it had really happened. The two brothers went on quietly with their experiments, making better and better aircraft and making longer and longer flights. Meanwhile, other people were also making aeroplanes.

The French were especially proud of their inventors and pilots. In 1907 Wilbur Wright came to France to demonstrate his aeroplane. It had to be carried in pieces in packing cases and then put together. Wilbur took so long over the work and was so quiet and shy that people began to laugh at him. However, on August 8th, 1908 thousands came to the race course at Le Mans to watch his test flight. He soared into the air, circled twice round the race course, did a figure of eight and came gracefully back to land. The crowd was amazed and delighted.

Back in the United States, Orville was also giving demonstrations. He flew over 250 feet high, and stayed up for well over an hour at a time. From then on the two quiet, modest brothers were famous, and they soon became rich as well.

What did Wilbur and Orville think their machines would do? For one thing, they hoped they would prevent wars. They thought that because generals would be able to fly over enemy lines and discover what was happening, they could ruin each other's plans quite easily, and no one would bother to fight any more. In fact, the aeroplane was to make war more horrible than it had ever been.

5 Across the Atlantic by Aeroplane

During the First World War aeroplanes had improved greatly. By the time it was over, there were thousands of military aircraft. Could aeroplanes be useful in peacetime? For a time it looked as if airships might be better. With their huge cigar-shaped envelopes full of gas, they carried much heavier loads than aeroplanes could. Passengers and crew travelled in comfort. If an engine failed the airship did not crash at once as an aeroplane did.

However, there were plenty of men, and even women, who were willing to take aeroplanes on long, dangerous flights. One of these was John Alcock. He had an exciting time as a pilot during the War. He shot down several enemy planes, but in the end he crashed on enemy territory and was taken prisoner by the Turks. He did not return home until the War ended in 1918. At that time, the Daily Mail was offering a prize of £10,000 to the first man to fly non-stop across the Atlantic. Alcock decided to try to win it, so he went to the firm of Vickers and

Alcock and Brown

persuaded them to give him one of their 'Vimy' bombers which had been built to bomb Berlin. In theory, the Vickers-Vimy could fly the Atlantic. But would it? So much depended on how well the aeroplane was built and how reliable its two Rolls Royce engines were. Alcock felt he was able to pilot the plane but he also needed a good navigator. One day, when he was at Vickers, a quiet, shy young man came into the room. He was Arthur Brown. Like Alcock he had been a pilot during the War. The two men began talking and, almost at once, Alcock knew that Brown was the right man to be his navigator.

The shortest distance across the Atlantic is from Newfoundland to Ireland. It was easier to fly from the American side, because then the prevailing westerly winds would help them. The Vimy bomber had to be taken apart and shipped to Newfoundland. Once there, mechanics worked hard to put it together, hindered much of the time by spectators. Some of them prodded the fabric of the aeroplane with umbrellas and one even tried to light it with a cigar! Another problem was to find an airstrip, for the country was wild and rocky. Alcock and Brown found a reasonable piece of land 400 yards long, but it was barely enough.

By June 14th, 1919 everything was ready. The aeroplane had made two test flights. Its petrol tanks had been filled and food had been packed for the journey — sandwiches, chocolate and thermos flasks of coffee. The passengers also went on board. They were two black cats called Lucky Jim and Twinkletoes.

Alcock and Brown were anxious to leave. A Major Brackley was also in Newfoundland busily preparing a big Handley Page aeroplane ready to attempt an Atlantic crossing. Alcock and Brown got up at 3.30 a.m., only to find a strong cross-wind was blowing. They waited for it to die down until finally they lost patience. At 5.28 p.m. they decided to go. Alcock raced the Vimy along the short runway and at the last second took her into the air. They just missed a fence, but beyond that was a wood. From the ground it looked as if they brushed the trees, but they cleared them by several feet. The long flight had begun.

the Vickers Vimy over the Atlantic

The two men sat side by side in their little cockpit. They were so cramped that at the end of the journey they said they wanted to stay standing for the rest of their lives. The whole time Alcock had to keep one hand on the joystick and both feet on the rudder bar. Brown had to concentrate on his charts and instruments and make difficult calculations. They could not speak because of the roar of the engines and the noise became even worse when an exhaust pipe melted away. They had a strong following wind, but in every other way the weather was unkind. They had rain, snow, sleet and hail. Several times Brown had to climb out of the cockpit and kneel on the fuselage to wipe snow from a gauge. The clouds shut out the sky so Brown could see neither sun nor stars to help him navigate. They climbed through a bank of cloud to find another above that and another above that again. Once they had to climb to 11,000 feet for a look at the sky. At that height the sleet jammed some of the controls and one of the engines made an alarming pop-pop-popping noise.

Their worst moment was when they suddenly hit a bank of fog. It was impossible to tell whether they were level or straight. The aeroplane stalled, then went into a spin. They knew they were falling simply because they were pressed against the backs of their seats. If the fog had gone down to sea level, they would certainly have crashed. Suddenly they broke clear of the fog and there was the sea, standing upright, or so it seemed. The aeroplane was flying on its side. Alcock straightened the plane just in time. They could even hear the sound of the waves above the noise of the engines.

At 8.15 the next morning they saw two small islands and soon they were circling round the little Irish village of Clifden. Alcock saw what he thought was a beautiful stretch of green field, and brought the aeroplane down for what would have been a perfect landing. Suddenly the machine jarred to a stop and its nose stuck in the ground. The beautiful green field was, in fact, an Irish bog. The time was 9.25 a.m. They had come 1,800 miles in just under sixteen hours.

Until then, hardly anyone had heard of Alcock and Brown, but now they were heroes. However, as Arthur Brown crawled out of his cockpit, dazed from the crash, and so stiff he could hardly walk, he was sure of one thing. If people were going to fly across the Atlantic, it would be far better to travel by airship.

6 Airships

In 1783 two Frenchmen, the Montgolfier brothers, made the first hot air balloon. They were too scared to go up in it themselves, so on its trial flight the balloon carried a sheep, a duck and a cockerel. In front of a large crowd, which included King Louis XVI and his Queen, these animals took off from Versailles near Paris. They were in the air for eight hours and flew two miles. Soon people found that hydrogen was more effective at lifting than hot air. During the nineteenth century there were many successful flights in hydrogen balloons. But the trouble with a balloon is that you have to go where the wind takes

the Montgolfier hot air balloon

you. People tried 'rowing' their balloons with huge, canvas covered oars. Then they tried propellors turned by hand. When they found that men were not strong enough to do this, they tried steam engines, but these were far too heavy. Then, in the 1880s Daimler made his petrol engine. Here, at last, was a machine that was powerful enough for air travel and not too heavy. At about the same time, scientists discovered how to produce aluminium cheaply. Now it was possible to make an airship. Instead of one balloon, they had several in a row. To stop them flopping all over the place, they put them in a huge framework of aluminium and covered it with fabric. Beneath this envelope, as it was called, were the motor and the 'gondola' which carried the passengers.

The most famous of the airship builders was a German, Count von Zeppelin, but the man we are going to meet is called Hugo Eckener. He worked for Zeppelin until the old man died in 1917. Then he became Chairman of the Company. We will visit him in 1935 and talk about his airship the *Graf Zeppelin*.

'*Why are you so keen on airships, Herr Eckener?*' 'Because they are the best way to travel. In the *Graf Zeppelin* we can go at 80 m.p.h. which is three times as fast as an ocean liner. The passengers are just as comfortable, too. There is plenty of room for them to stretch their legs, and there is always something interesting to see from the windows. The world looks wonderful from up there. I shall always remember a sight-seeing trip we made in 1928. We went to the South of France and from there to Rome. Then we flew over Crete, Cyprus and Palestine. We flew very slowly whenever we saw anything of interest. I took the ship low over the Dead Sea. The passengers were amazed when I told them we were flying 1,000 feet *below* sea level! We came back to Germany over the Austrian Alps. We had travelled for three days without stopping. Everyone was delighted.'

'*Flying over the sea cannot be very interesting.*' 'No, but we can cross the Atlantic in a couple of days. We have an orchestra to keep people amused and an excellent kitchen so we can serve very good meals.' '*What happens in a storm?*' 'That can be exciting. Rain or hail beating on the envelope makes a tremendous noise, and the ship pitches and rolls. The cups and

building an airship

the Hindenburg

plates often fly off the tables. Still, it's no worse than being on a lincr.' *It's more dangerous, surely.'* 'We could never have an airship disaster as great as the sinking of the *Titanic,* because airships couldn't carry so many passengers' replies Herr Eckener. 'And airships are much safer than aeroplanes. If the engines of an aeroplane fail, it crashes at once. An airship will at least stay up if the engines fail. If we have a fault on the *Graf Zeppelin* we can sometimes put it right without landing. If we can't put it right, we can just float gently down to earth.'

'Yes, but several airships have crashed, and if the hydrogen explodes everyone aboard is killed. The British haven't flown airships since the R.101 crashed.' 'Well, we have overcome those problems in our new ship the *Hindenburg.* We shall fill her with helium, which is much safer than hydrogen. The only problem is that we have to get helium from America. I don't know whether America will let us have any more. They

don't trust Germany now that Hitler is in power. I can't blame them. I don't like Hitler myself.'

This new airship, the *Hindenburg,* was the finest ever built. She was 800 feet long, with four huge diesel engines, each over 1,000 h.p., and she could carry fifty passengers. The *Hindenburg* had a lounge, a library, a promenade deck, a dining room and luxurious cabins, each with a bathroom. Unfortunately, as Hugo Eckener feared, the Americans refused to sell helium to Germany. The *Hindenburg* had to use hydrogen after all. She began flying in 1936, and made several trips to the United States and South America. Everyone said she was a great success. Then, on May 6th, 1937 she arrived at Lakehurst near New York. A radio commentator called Herb Morrison was there to broadcast what was happening although it was not expected to be very exciting. This is what he said: 'Passengers are looking out of the windows waving. The ship is standing still now. The vast motors are just holding it, just enough to keep it from . . .' Suddenly he shouted, 'It's broken into flames. It's flashing! Flashing! It's flashing terribly! It's bursting into flames and falling on the mooring mast. This is terrible. This is one of the worst catastrophes in the world. Oh, the humanity and all the passengers . . . I told you . . . it's a mass of smoking wreckage. . . I . . . I . . . folks, I'm going to have to stop for a moment because I've lost my voice. This is the worst thing I have ever witnessed.'

There were 97 people on board and 35 of them died. After the loss of the *Hindenburg* no one wanted to travel by airship again. No one knows for certain why the *Hindenburg* exploded. Possibly a charge of static electricity ignited the hydrogen, which is a highly inflammable gas.

The Hindenburg

7 Scott of the Antarctic

The southern continent of Antarctica is a huge plateau, covered almost entirely with snow and ice. It is terribly cold, there are howling blizzards, and for four months of the year there is complete darkness. In the early twentieth century, people began to explore Antarctica. Why was this? For one thing, scientists wanted to study the rocks, the weather, the movement of ice, the earth's magnetic field and the strange creatures, such as the Emperor Penguins, which lived there. The main reason, though, was to find adventure, and to go where no one had been before. Above all, they wanted to reach the South Pole. The first person to do so would certainly become famous.

One of the most enthusiastic explorers of the southern continent was Robert Falcon Scott, a captain in the Royal Navy. In 1901 he led an expedition in the *Discovery*. Quite possibly you have seen her, for she is now moored on the Embankment in London.

Captain Scott

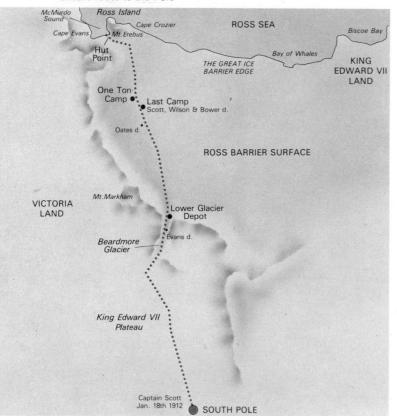

Scott's route to the Pole

Scott did not try to reach the South Pole on that expedition, but he did learn a lot about living and working in Antarctica. In 1910, he set sail again, this time in the *Terra Nova*. She was a whaling ship which had been built for the Southern Ocean, so she was just right for the expedition.

If you look at the map of Antarctica, you will notice a huge bay by the Ross Sea. It looks as if it is possible to sail quite close to the South Pole. But this bay is covered with ice hundreds of feet thick. Explorers called it the Great Ice Barrier. The *Terra Nova* could go no further than Ross Island. Scott and his men built themselves a wooden house at the foot of a smouldering volcano they named Mount Erebus. Here they spent the winter. They found plenty of scientific work to do and they thought about the problems and dangers of the journey that lay ahead. Their biggest worry was that they were not alone. On one of their scientific trips the crew of the *Terra Nova* were amazed to find another ship. She was called the *Fram* and she carried an expedition led by the famous Norwegian explorer, Amundsen. Amundsen was determined to reach the South Pole before Scott.

Mount Erebus from Hut Point, a watercolour by Dr. Wilson

Scott and his friends waited impatiently for the summer, which of course comes to countries south of the equator during our winter. At last, on November 1st, 1911, they set out. The plan was to start with a large party carrying as many supplies as possible. Every 65 miles or so they made a depot of stores that could be used on the return journey. The further they went, the less there was to carry, so Scott sent back

Captain Scott writing his diary in the hut

three groups of men at different times. They were bitterly disappointed because they were not allowed to go to the Pole. To pull their sledges Scott's team had ponies, dogs and two tractors with petrol engines. The motors broke down after only fifty miles. The wretched ponies struggled through the snow until they were too weak to go any further, and had to be shot. With the journey about half finished, Scott sent back the dog teams. There was now only one way to pull the sledges. The men had to do it themselves.

By this time they had travelled 450 miles over the Great Ice Barrier to reach the foot of the plateau. A great river of ice, the Beardmore Glacier, lay ahead. The glacier is twenty miles wide in places and it is 120 miles long, rising to 10,000 feet at the top of the plateau. All over the glacier are great ridges, so hauling the sledges was very hard work for Scott and his men. It was dangerous as well, because of crevasses. These are wide, deep cracks in the ice, and it is usually impossible to see them because the snow makes a kind of bridge over the top. On an earlier trip, Scott had seen a whole team of dogs vanish into a crevasse, one after the other. This time a member of his party fell through one and found himself dangling

7 Scott of the Antarctic

Manhauling a sledge over the ice-cap

at the end of his harness with an 80 foot drop below him.

It took the expedition three weeks to climb to the top of the glacier, and then Scott sent back his last return party. He pressed on with only four men, Dr. Wilson, Captain Oates, Petty Officer Evans and Lieutenant Bowers. Tugging the heavy sledges was hard, tiring work and their strength began to fail. However, the thought of being the first men at the South Pole kept them going. At last, when they were only a day's march from their goal, one of them saw a black dot on the horizon. As they drew nearer, they soon realized the worst. It was the Norwegian flag they could see. Amundsen had placed it there thirty-three days before. The five tired, disappointed Englishmen now faced the 800 mile tramp back to their base camp.

The biting winds tore at their faces until they were covered in sores. Petty Officer Evans's finger nails began falling off. Edward Wilson suffered from snow blindness, and strained a muscle in his leg. Scott fell and hurt his shoulder. In three weeks they managed to reach the top of the Beardmore Glacier. Then began the most difficult part of their journey, picking their way among the great ridges and crevasses. Petty Officer Evans was a giant of a man, full of good humour, but he was worn out and so confused as the result of a fall that he could not even do up his boots properly. He died on February 17th.

Scott's exhausted party at the Pole *left to right* Oates, Bowers, Scott, Evans, Wilson

the Great Ice Barrier *right* the last entry in Scott's diary

The rest of the party struggled to the foot of the glacier and then a further 250 miles over the Great Ice Barrier. At last they made camp, not knowing that a relief party was only eleven miles away. Captain Oates was now very ill, and knew he was a burden to the others. While a blizzard was raging, he left the tent saying, 'I am just going outside and may be some time.' They never saw him again. The blizzard lasted for eight days, and when it was over Scott and his companions were too weak to move. They died where they lay.

Eight months later, a search party noticed a dark speck in the snow. It was the top of the tent. Inside were the bodies of the three explorers and also the diary that Scott had faithfully kept. It told the dreadful story of all the hardships and disappointment.

23

8 Everest

Everest from the air

If you tried to climb Everest you would find it rather like storming an enemy fortress. What problems would you face?

In the first place, there is the height. Everest is 29,002 feet high, which is more than six times as high as Ben Nevis. Up there, the cold is biting. If you are caught without shelter for the night you would certainly die. However, you can only carry a light tent which gives you barely enough protection from the cold. In addition, the air is thin. There is a good chance that you will suffer from 'anoxia' which means 'oxygen shortage'. This makes you violently sick and too weak to move. Even if that does not happen, you find that every step you take needs a great effort. You take two steps and have to rest, two steps more and have to rest again, and every ten steps or so you will fall down exhausted. You may behave very strangely. A member of the expedition in 1953 went to sleep with a sardine hanging out of his mouth! Your mind does not guide your body properly. At sea level you can light a stove and boil water in a couple of minutes. Up on Everest it may take you half an hour. You need a lot of liquids, too, because your body loses moisture very quickly. Everything

freezes solid, so you have to heat all your drinks. At least the melted snow is pure water!

The weather is certain to be bad for much of the time. You will have such severe snow storms that you will be unable to leave your camp, and if you are caught in a storm you may be lost for ever. The wind will howl almost without ceasing, and at night your tent will bang and thrash like the sail of a ship in a gale.

Now let us look at the mountain to see what you have to climb.

the Khumbu icefall

the route to the summit

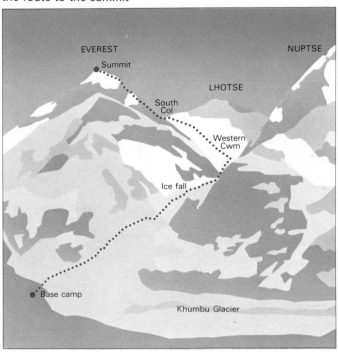

Everywhere in the Himalayas there are rivers, but they are rivers of ice, called glaciers. In places they are hundreds of feet thick, and up to two miles wide. They have gouged great valleys, and at their sources they have bitten back into the mountains, much as you would bite into an apple. A 'bite' like this is called a cwm, and there is one on Everest called the Western Cwm. On leaving it, the glacier drops suddenly into the valley below. It is not a waterfall, but an enormous icefall 2,000 feet high. The ice moves only a few feet a day, but it is alarming when it does. Sometimes there are cracks and groans, sometimes dull thuds, and sometimes a roaring like an express train, all caused by the movement of the ice. Everywhere there are huge boulders of ice, and even cliffs. Towering above you are ice pinnacles, some of which are likely to fall at any minute. At your feet you are likely to find a crack, or a crevasse. As the glacier leaves the cwm it has to bend, so it cracks open, just as your rubber does if you bend it over the corner of your desk. A crevasse can be a hundred feet deep. It may be so narrow that you can step over it quite easily, or it may be thirty feet wide.

Once you are in the Western Cwm you will find it is fairly flat, but at the far end is the Lhotse face. It is 4,000 feet high and almost as steep as a wall. Once up there, you come to the South Col. Here you will find a small area of flat land where you can camp. But the Col is a desolate and windswept place. From here you must climb to the South Summit, where you will see the way to the very top of Everest. It is above a knife-edge of rock with a drop of thousands of feet on either side.

How can mountaineers overcome all these problems? The most important things they need are great courage and determination. Next, they must have a lot of equipment and porters to carry it. Lastly, they must plan everything with immense care.

Several expeditions went to Everest, and in 1952 some Swiss mountaineers nearly reached the top. In 1953, Colonel John Hunt took a British party to the mountain. There were thirteen men altogether. Among them was a tall, lanky New Zealander called Edmund Hillary. Hillary kept bees for a living, but he was an expert mountaineer who had done a lot of climbing in New Zealand and in the Himalayas.

To help them carry all their food and equipment the British hired no less than 350 Sherpas. The Sherpas are a people who live in the mountains near Everest. Most of them are small, but they are courageous, very strong and are used to the cold and bad weather. They are also cheerful, loyal and hardworking. But the Sherpas lead a simple life and are not used to mechanical things. They found it impossible to learn how to use oxygen sets. They could light a paraffin stove, but the tea they brewed tasted horrible and was often thick with grease. On Everest, though, any warm drink is welcome.

Of course, not all 350 Sherpas were going to climb Everest. Most of them just carried their loads to the foot of the mountain and then went home. A few hand-picked ones who were expert climbers stayed. Among them was Tensing who had climbed with the Swiss party the year before. He and one of the Swiss had nearly reached the top.

The first stage of the journey was a hike of 170 miles through Nepal. It is beautiful, thickly wooded country but there are no roads, only a path which led the party over one mountain ridge after another. When they caught their first sight of Everest, some of them were so excited they climbed trees to have a better look. At last they arrived at the monastery of Thyangboche which has a grandstand view of the mountain. From here it was only a few days trek to the foot of the icefall.

a camp en route to Everest

Everest from Thyangboche Monastery

Everest

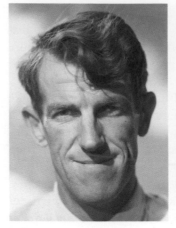

Hillary

Tensing

The only way to climb the mountain was to attempt it in stages. They had to set up camp after camp, each higher than the one before. The last camp had to be close enough to the top for the climbers to reach the summit and return safely in a day.

The first problem was to find a way up the icefall. Edmund Hillary led a party to do this. They picked their way among ice boulders and tottering ice pillars. They crossed, or dodged round, gaping crevasses and they scaled ice cliffs. All the time, the ice groaned and grumbled. They named various places – Mike's Horror, Hillary's Horror, Hell Fire Alley, Atom Bomb Area and Ghastly Crevasse. But in the end, they reached the cwm. Getting back to camp was unpleasant, but now it had been climbed once, the icefall did not seem to be so terrible after all.

Some members of the party then made the path as easy as they could. They bridged crevasses with wooden planks, they chopped steps, they fixed ropes to the sides of cliffs, and, at one point, they hung a rope ladder. They also marked the path with flags. The movement of the glacier and fresh falls of snow kept spoiling their work, but the Sherpas were able to carry load after load of supplies into the Western Cwm. Here they set up their advanced camp.

The next step was to find a way up the sheer wall of the Lhotse face. After several days they managed this and again they prepared the way with fixed ropes and steps. Not surprisingly, it was hard to persuade some of the Sherpas to carry their loads up there. But on May 21st, they finally pitched Camp 8 on the South Col.

Hunt had chosen two assault teams for the final attack. The first was Charles Evans and Tom Bourdillon; the other was Edmund Hillary and Tensing. On May 26th, Evans and Bourdillon set out. At first all went well, and the men below watched them with excitement. Only Tensing was silent. He thought a Sherpa should be one of the first men to climb to the top. By one o'clock Evans and Bourdillon had reached the South Summit. They could now see the very peak of the mountain and it was only 400 yards away. Should they go on? Unfortunately they were already tired and they were fast running out of oxygen. Probably they could have reached the top, but they knew that if they did so they would die on their way back down. At six o'clock they staggered into Camp 8, barely able to walk, with their faces covered in frost. It was now the turn of Hillary and Tensing.

On May 27th the weather was so bad they could do nothing. But on the following day they set out. Three other men came with them to carry their tent, spare oxygen and food. The five men climbed until mid-afternoon and then looked for a place to camp. The slopes were so steep that it seemed impossible to find one, but in the end they discovered a ledge, a tiny shelf on the face of a precipice, thousands of feet high. The three companions turned back, leaving the equipment they had carried, including a large cylinder of oxygen. This was the supply Hillary and Tensing needed for the night. It is impossible to sleep at that height without oxygen.

The ledge had a slope of 30 degrees, so Hillary and Tensing levelled it as well as they could, prising rocks out of the frozen ground. The ground was too hard

climbers on Everest

a high camp on Everest

for tent pegs, so they stuck oxygen bottles in the snow and used those. When they had put the tent up they had supper of soup, sardines on biscuits, dates and pint after pint of sweet lemonade. They also ate a tin of apricots which Hillary had kept hidden until then. It was a great treat.

The night was miserable. Every now and then a gust of wind threatened to blow them off their ledge. They also found that one of their helpers had taken back the adaptor for the large bottle of oxygen. They only dared use their climbing oxygen for four hours, so they had little sleep.

At 6.30 the next morning they set off. It was a hard struggle to reach the South Summit, and after that came the dreadful ridge that had defeated Bourdillon and Evans. The only way was to chip steps all the way up it. They went over one hump after another, hoping each would be the last, but the ridge seemed to go on for ever. At one point they reached a sheer wall forty feet high. It looked impossible, but it had a crack in it and they were able to force their way up that. At 11.30 a.m. they finally reached the summit.

What do you do at the top of Everest? Hillary and Tensing shook hands, like the English, then hugged one another like Sherpas. Tensing buried a few sweets and chocolates as an offering to the gods that live on the mountain, and Hillary buried a little white crucifix. Hillary next took some photographs of the mountains all around, then three of Tensing. There is no photograph of Hillary on the summit because Tensing did not know how to use a camera and Hillary thought it was hardly the time to teach him. After a quarter of an hour they made their way down. They reached the South Col by the evening, just as the oxygen ran out. The following morning they arrived in the Western Cwm, so all

Tensing on the summit

they had to do was to go down the icefall for the last time and make the long hike through Nepal.

The expedition had been a great success, and everyone had shown tremendous skill and courage. Both Hunt and Hillary were knighted. But why had they wanted to reach the top of Everest in the first place? The only answer Sir John Hunt could give was, 'We climbed it because it was there.'

Work Section

Understand Your Work

1 Ocean Liners
1 Who invented the steam turbine?
2 In what ways was it better than an ordinary steam engine?
3 Why was the Cunard Company interested in the steam turbine?
4 How many funnels has the *Mauretania*? Why is the number important?
5 What rooms are there in the *Mauretania*?
6 How do the passengers spend their time?
7 How many miles can the *Mauretania* sail in a day? How long does it take her to cross the Atlantic?
8 Why are third class passengers more likely to be seasick than those travelling first class?
9 What fuel does the *Mauretania* burn?
10 What kind of men are stokers?

2 The First Motor Cars
1 What inventions, made before 1800, were later used in motor cars?
2 How was Lenoir's engine driven? Why was it better than a steam engine?
3 What is benzine? What did oil companies do with it in the early days? Why?
4 Who invented the first petrol engine? When?
5 What law made life difficult for early motorists in Britain?
6 Why was there a celebration drive from London to Brighton in 1896?
7 Why has Dr. Bulleid bought a car?
8 What problems is his car likely to give him?
9 What problems does it give other people?
10 How are roads being improved in some areas?

3 The Austin Seven
1 When were the first Austin Sevens made?
2 How many people could ride in one, in comfort?
3 How did the Austin Seven compare with bigger cars?
4 How reliable was it?
5 Why did Mrs. Brown not want her husband to buy a motor bike and sidecar?
6 What difference could an Austin Seven make to the life of an ordinary family?
7 Where were Austin Sevens made?
8 What did the factory produce when it first opened?
9 Why did Sir Herbert Austin decide to make Austin Sevens?
10 Where did George Simpson drive an Austin Seven in 1928?

4 The First Aeroplanes
1 How did people first try to fly? Name two methods.
2 What did Sir George Cayley discover?
3 Name one of the first successful glider pilots.
4 Why was the invention of the petrol engine important?
5 Where did the Wright brothers live?
6 Where did they carry out their experiments? Why?
7 What did they practise before they tried powered flight?
8 When was their first powered flight? How long did it last?
9 Where did Wilbur and Orville make demonstration flights? What did they do on these flights?
10 What effect did the Wright brothers think their invention would have on war?

5 Across the Atlantic by Aeroplane
1 Why did airships seem better than aeroplanes for long distance flights?
2 Why did John Alcock decide to fly the Atlantic? What aeroplane did he use? Why had it been built?
3 What help did John Alcock want from Arthur Brown?
4 Where did they fly from? Why?
5 When did Alcock and Brown take off?
6 In what ways was the flight uncomfortable?
7 What dangers did they face?
8 Why was it necessary to climb to 11,000 feet?
9 Where did they land? How long had the flight taken?
10 What conclusion did Arthur Brown draw from the flight? Why?

6 Airships
1 When was the first balloon flight? What were the passengers?
2 Describe two ways of filling a balloon. Which seemed the better way?
3 What ways of driving balloons did people try? Which method succeeded?
4 How was an airship different in construction from a balloon? What metal was used?
5 Who was the most famous of the airship builders?
6 How fast could an airship travel? How long did one take to cross the Atlantic?
7 Why was it pleasant to travel on an airship?
8 What was particularly dangerous about airships?
9 Why did the Germans want to use helium in the *Hindenburg*? Why was this not possible?
10 What happened to the *Hindenburg*? How did this affect travel by airship?

7 Scott of the Antarctic
1 What is unpleasant about the continent of Antarctica?
2 What scientific reasons were there for exploring it?
3 Give the dates of Scott's two expeditions and the names of the ships he sailed in.
4 Why could the expedition sail no further than Ross Island? What did Scott's party do there?
5 When did the expedition leave for the South Pole?
6 What ways did they have of pulling their sledges?
7 What dangers did they face on the Beardmore Glacier?
8 What did Scott discover at the South Pole?
9 Describe Captain Oates's brave action.

28

10 What happened to Scott and his other companions? How do we know about their journey?

8 Everest
1 How high is Everest?
2 How does the weather cause problems for climbers?
3 How does the thin air affect them?
4 Why is it difficult and dangerous to climb a glacier? (See also section 7.)
5 Name the stages to the top of Everest, after leaving the glacier.
6 What equipment do climbers need?
7 Who led the British expedition in 1953? How many men were in the party?
8 Who are Sherpas? Why did the expedition need them?
9 Name one of the Sherpas. What had he done in 1952?
10 Where did the expedition make its base camp?
11 How did they overcome the difficulties on the glacier?
12 Which two men first tried to reach the summit? Why did they fail?
13 Which two men finally reached the summit?
14 What did they do there?
15 What reason was given for climbing Everest?

Use Your Imagination

The figures in brackets tell you which section will help you answer the question.
1 It is 1900. You have heard that the Cunard Company is planning to build a new liner. Write a letter to the Directors persuading them to use turbines to drive her. (You will have to explain what a turbine is, if they are to understand your letter.) (1)
2 You have crossed the Atlantic as a first class passenger in the *Mauretania*. Write a description of the voyage. (1)
3 It is 1910. A motorist has an argument with someone who dislikes cars. Describe what they say. (2)
4 Write the life story of one of the early motor cars. (2, 3)
5 It is 1928. You are the owner of a Rolls Royce. Write what you think about Austin Sevens. (3)
6 It is 1930. Write a report for a newspaper on how you think the motor car is changing people's lives. What dangers can you see in the future? (2, 3)
7 It is December 14th, 1903 and you are at Kill Devil Hill. Give a running commentary on what happens. (4)
8 You are John Alcock. Say why you think it is possible to cross the Atlantic by aeroplane, and explain why you wish to do it. (5)
9 You have just made a flight by airship. Say what the airship was like, and write a description of the flight. (6)
10 It is 1920. Write a letter to a newspaper saying why you

think it will be better for Great Britain to build airships rather than aeroplanes. (5, 6)
11 How might transport have developed if no one had invented the petrol engine? (2–6)
12 You are Captain Scott. Write a list of the equipment you will carry on the *Terra Nova* for your expedition to the South Pole. (7)
13 You are Captain Oates. Write your diary for the journey to the South Pole. At the end explain why you are going to walk out into the blizzard. (7)
14 Two people discuss the Everest expedition. One is in favour of it and one is against it. Write out their argument. (8)
15 List the ways in which transport has been improved in the twentieth century. Which development do you think has been the most important, and why?
What further changes do you think are going to take place in your lifetime? (All sections)

Further Work

1 Read more about the great liners of the early twentieth century, foreign, as well as British.
What was the fate of the *Titanic*, the *Lusitania* and the *Queen Elizabeth I*?
Why are ocean liners less common today?
2 Collect pictures of early motor cars and, if possible, visit a motor museum.
List the ways in which motor cars have improved since the early twentieth century.
3 What is 'ribbon development'? How did the motor car help to bring it about?
4 Write an account of forms of road transport other than the motor car, e.g. buses and lorries. Include something on the diesel engine.
5 Find out what you can about the aeroplanes of the First World War.
6 Read about other pioneers of long distance flying, e.g. Keith and Ross Smith, Charles Lindbergh and Amy Johnson.
7 Read more about airships, e.g. Zeppelins in the First World War, and the loss of the R.101.
8 Read the stories of other voyages of exploration to the polar regions, the North Pole, as well as the South Pole.
9 What expeditions were made to Everest before 1953? Why did they fail?
10 Write a short history of space travel.

Chapter Two At School and at Work

1 The Elementary School

We are back in the 1890s and Weymouth House School in Bath has just had a new building. It is plain, but so solid that it will last for a hundred years or more. It has three storeys. The ground floor is for infants, the first floor is for girls and the top floor is for boys. On each floor there is a large hall as big as a modern gymnasium. This is called the school room and Mr. Swanson, the headmaster of the boys' school, says there are three standards in this room.

'*What are standards, Mr. Swanson?*' 'They are classes. There are about forty boys in each. Standard One is for boys aged seven, Standard Two is for boys aged eight and so on. A boy has to pass an examination before he can go up a Standard. Some boys spend their whole school life in Standard One. A bright lad can jump a standard. Pupils are allowed to leave as soon as they have passed Standard Four, otherwise they have to stay at school until they are twelve. Many play truant, of course. Some parents send their sons to work in their last year. The magistrates fine them, half-a-crown perhaps, but the boys' wages soon pay that.'

a new school in the nineteenth century

'*Don't the classes disturb each other, Mr. Swanson?*' 'They do a little, but this way I can keep an eye on the boys and on the teachers. We have two classrooms as well. Standard Four is in one of them and Standards Five and Six are in the other.'

The two classrooms have glass screens, so in fact Mr. Swanson can see what is happening in them nearly as well as he can in the schoolroom.

'*Your teachers look young, Headmaster.*' 'They are not as young as they would have been in years gone by. At one time a headmaster had only monitors to help him, and they were children of twelve or so. Mr. King, Mr. Budd and Miss Edwards are all over eighteen. The youngest here is my pupil teacher, Stephen Dunton. He is only fourteen, but I don't give him much to do. I take two standards myself, and he helps me.'

'*What subjects do you teach?*' 'This is a Church school, so religion is very important. The trouble is that religion does not earn grant, so I teach it first thing in the morning when all the latecomers are arriving. Then I mark the register. What really matters are the three Rs — reading, writing and arithmetic.' '*What is this grant?*' 'Every year we have a visit from an inspector. He gives the boys an examination, and if they do well the Government gives the school managers money. A good boy can earn the school over a pound a year. The rich people of Bath still give money to the school, but most of it comes from the Government these days. If the grant is too low, the managers might not have enough cash to pay my salary. I make the boys work, believe me.'

'*Do you teach only the three Rs?*' 'Oh no. We can earn grant for singing, drawing, and what we call class subjects. In this school the class subjects are history, geography and object lessons.'

'*You have no piano for teaching music, I notice.*' Mr. Swanson takes a tuning fork from his desk. 'The boys can earn the music grant if they can sing a couple of easy songs by ear. All I have to do is start

them on the right note, and I don't need a piano to play one note.'

'*What are object lessons?*' Mr. Swanson takes us into one of the classrooms where Standard One is listening to the pupil teacher, Stephen Dunton. He is sharpening a pencil and telling the children that he can cut the wood quite easily. He then asks if anyone knows what kind of wood it is. A few boys give wrong answers so Stephen tells them that it is cedar wood and that cedar trees grow in the Lebanon. One of the boys asks what that is, but Stephen pretends not to hear and goes on to talk about the pencil lead.

'Object lessons teach the boys to observe and reason,' says Mr. Swanson. 'Here are the object lessons for Standard One. There are all sorts of things on this list: a bucket, a camel, rain, an orange and so on.' *Are object lessons a kind of science, then?*' 'You could say that,' replies Mr. Swanson.

He now shows us some drawings. They are the most intricate patterns and beautifully drawn, but all copied from a book, so we ask if the boys do any imaginative work. 'The purpose of drawing is to train the hand and the eye,' says Mr. Swanson. 'The imagination is something we have to keep in check.' At this moment a boy appears. He stands to attention and salutes, saying that Mr. King had sent him for the cane. Mr. Swanson canes him twice on each hand, and a hush falls over the school. '*You believe in being firm, Headmaster!*' 'If the boys behave badly they will not learn their lessons properly. Besides, there is a grant of 1/6d per head for discipline.'

2 The Boarding School

Charles Walker

Charles Walker, who is fourteen, lives in Bath but he goes to a boarding school at Blandford in Dorset. It is quite easy to get there because it is near the Somerset and Dorset Railway which runs from Green Park Station in Bath to Bournemouth.

In those days everyone admired the old and very famous schools, such as Eton and Harrow. They are called public schools, though in fact they are so expensive that only rich people can afford the fees. Charles's school is neither old nor famous. but it tries to copy them. For one thing, it is divided into houses. You may have a house system at your school, but in this boarding school the boys really do live in separate houses. A housemaster has charge of each one and does all he can to see that his boys are the best in the school at work and at games.

First, we will meet the headmaster who will tell us about his ideas on education.

'My main aim is to train the character of my boys. I have to turn them into gentlemen and leaders. I don't believe in being soft with them. We have discipline here and if a boy misbehaves, I give him a good hiding. We have no fancy food, just good plain meals. To harden the boys we make them take a cold bath every morning, winter and summer. They have games most afternoons, rugby in winter and cricket in summer. If they cannot play because of the weather, then we send them for a good long cross-country run. I believe in team games because they teach boys to take knocks and to be unselfish. The

house system helps a lot. Boys are keen for their house to win, so they play hard. We have prefects, of course. They have their own bedrooms, a special table in hall, their own uniform and other privileges. They help with the discipline of the school and I allow them to cane the younger boys, if they think it necessary. Every senior boy has a junior to fag for him. The senior learns how to give orders, and the junior learns how to obey them. I am a clergyman of the Church of England, so I take chapel every morning, and Communion and Evensong on Sundays. My sermons do much to guide and inspire the boys. We have to train their minds as well as their characters, of course. The boys learn useful subjects, like English and mathematics, but their real education comes from the Classics, Latin and Greek.'

'*Isn't it important to learn science these days, Headmaster?*' 'Oh, we do teach some science, but that is strictly for boys who are not very bright. Science is all very well for those who are unfortunate enough to have to work in industry, but our glorious Empire is ruled by men trained in the Classics.'

We will now see what Charles says about his school.

'I hate it here. Papa says that school days are the best days of your life but I don't believe him. What would he say to a cold bath on a January morning? The food is dreadful, not much more than bread and butter with some meat and potatoes at lunch. Luckily there is a tuck shop in Blandford. We go there whenever we can and have steak and onion, ham and eggs, mushrooms on toast and puddings and cakes. I quite like cricket in the summer and rugby isn't too bad, except that we get caked in mud and have to wash in cold water. There is too much fuss about which house wins. What I like best are the boxing and fencing in the gymnasium. We have an army sergeant who takes us and I think he is a better teacher than the masters.'

'*What do you think about the prefect system?*' 'I hate prefects. They are sneaks and bullies. They have their own rooms with fires in the winter, while we sleep in a cold dormitory. I have to fag for Jones, which means I have to tidy his room, make him scrambled eggs on toast and that sort of thing. If he wants a bit of fun he twists my ears, or holds me close to his fire until I scream. But I will have my own fag one day. Then I will get my revenge.'

'*Do you enjoy your lessons, Charles?*' 'Not at all, as we don't do much but boring old Latin and Greek. We are translating reams of Virgil at the moment.

Luckily one of my friends has a crib.' '*What is that?*' 'It is an English translation. We just copy it and make a few mistakes so that it looks like our own work. But the most boring thing is having to go to chapel and listen to old Porky's sermons. I try to sit where he can't see me dozing off.'

'*What do you want to do when you leave school?*' 'I want to be an engineer. I want to design steam turbines, like Parsons. His name is Charles, the same as mine. Papa and Mama won't hear of it, though, and I dare not tell anyone at school. The trouble is that the things they are teaching me here will not be the least bit of use. But I must go now. Mama promised to send me a hamper, and with any luck it will be waiting for me in the porter's lodge.'

3 Secondary Education for All

A middle aged man will tell us about his school days. He came from a poor home, but he is now a wealthy solicitor. He has done well in life because he went to a secondary school. Today, everyone has a secondary education, but when this man was young, only a few children had the opportunity. They were the lucky ones who had passed a difficult examination, or whose parents could afford school fees.

'One winter morning, back in 1937, I was just leaving for school when my mother called me. She told me to open my mouth, and then gave me a spoonful of Glucose-D. This was a sickly-sweet white powder which clung to the inside of your mouth. On the tin, it said it gave you strength and energy. Normally, we only took it when we were ill, so I was surprised. But this was no ordinary morning. I was going to sit my scholarship examination.

'There were three schools in our little town – Brookside, High Street and Weston Hill. The first two were much the same. I went to Brookside, which was an old building with pointed gables, a slate roof, and a turret with an iron bell. The bell rope had been broken for years, but that did not matter because the teachers used whistles. There was a central hall, with classrooms around it. The floors were so worn it was

Poole's Park School football team in 1938

impossible to clean them. When we stamped applause at Christmas concerts the air filled with dust. The school was cold. Every winter playtime rows of boys clustered round the huge iron pipes that carried lukewarm water round the building. There were no laboratories, no workshops, and no domestic science rooms. This was an elementary school, built in about 1860 to teach the children of the poor their three Rs – reading, writing and arithmetic; even in 1937 little more was taught. I had started at Brookside when I was five. I was now eleven and I expected to stay until I was fourteen. The only question was whether I could "pass my scholarship".

'The only children who had a chance of passing were in Miss Evitt's scholarship class. She had worked hard with us, but even so, we knew that only five or six could pass. Her way of teaching mental arithmetic was to stand us round the room while she barked questions at us in turn. If we answered wrongly, she swished us with her cane. She had the best scholarship results in our part of the county and meant to keep it that way.

'The scholarship examination had three parts. There was an English test, an arithmetic test, and a test on general knowledge. I went home without hope, and the rest of the term passed quietly. Then it happened. During the Easter holidays a letter came from the County Council which told my parents I had been awarded a Free Place at Weston Hill Secondary School. I went upstairs, knelt by my bed and said a prayer of thanks to God. I should have thanked Miss Evitt as well.

'As a pupil at Weston Hill, I was rather superior. My grandfather bought me a new bicycle – a shining "Hercules" which cost at least £3. My parents bought me the school uniform, and a big, strong leather satchel. My father painted my initials on it in small, neat black letters.

'Weston Hill was a very different school from Brookside. The floors were polished, and the brass door handles shone. There were a dozen well-heated classrooms, an assembly hall, and a gymnasium. Behind the main school was a brand new concrete building which housed laboratories, physics down-

nearly as difficult. We called it the "eleven plus", because children took it when they were eleven or just over. My younger brother failed this selection test. In the old days my grandfather would probably have paid his fees to Weston Hill, but this was no longer allowed. However much the family disliked the idea, Dennis had to go to Brookside Secondary Modern. When I asked him what it was like, he said that it was the same old gang teaching the same old rubbish. Most people felt things were much as before. Miss Evitt coached and caned children for the "11 +", just as she had done for the scholarship. In fact, she continued to talk about her "scholarship winners" until the day she retired.

post-war schoolboys

stairs and chemistry upstairs. There were also rooms for woodwork and housecraft, but no one took these subjects seriously. Latin, French and science were going to be far more important in our lives. At first, we couldn't see much sense in learning Latin, but I am glad I took it, because I needed it to go to university.

'The children came from elementary and private schools from miles around. One girl rode to school on a horse. The "scholarship winners" were placed in Form One Parallel. We were told we were the brighter pupils but that if we did not work hard we would go down to Form One. The children in Form One had not passed the scholarship examination so their parents had to pay fees. Many of them had come from a small private school in the town where pupils did not learn much, but they did not have to mix with the miners' children in the elementary schools. For their parents this was more important than anything else.

After the War and the Education Act of 1944 the schools changed, especially High Street and Brookside. All the younger children went to High Street, which was made a Primary School. The older ones went to Brookside, which was called a Secondary Modern School. As for Weston Hill, it became a Grammar School and still took the best pupils. There was no "scholarship examination", it is true, but there was a "secondary selection test" which was

'It is different today. Weston Hill Grammar School has become Weston Hill Comprehensive School and the old red brick building is surrounded with extensions. Brookside has handsome new buildings on a new site, and is also a comprehensive school. Pupils attend one or the other, depending only on where they live and not whether thay can pass an examination. However, those of us who were pupils at Weston Hill would still prefer our children to go to that school.'

4 The Trawler Skipper

It is 1960. We will go to Hull to talk to George Hume, who is the skipper of a trawler. He has just come back from a voyage. His ship, the *City of Nottingham* is nearly 200 feet long and carries a crew of twenty. You can see from the diagram how she catches fish. The map shows you where the fishing grounds are. The best ones are in the shallower waters, near land.

'How long have you been at sea, Mr. Hume?' 'We have had an average trip – about three weeks. We have been to Iceland. It usually takes us seven days to go there, and seven days to come home, and we spend seven days on the fishing grounds. We have two or three days ashore, then off we go again.' *'Did*

a fishing fleet in harbour

you catch many fish?' 'Enough. This cargo is worth about £6,000 – that's about 150 tons of cod.'

'What is it like on voyage?' 'Well, the trip out isn't usually too bad. The crew have no more to do than if they were on a cargo boat. The work really begins when we start to fish. We work round the clock, and no man has more than six hours sleep in twenty-four. Usually we trawl for about two and a half hours, then up comes the net, full of cod, with any luck. We tip them all over the deck, and the men have to work frantically to get the net back over the side. Sometimes it's quite badly torn. As soon as we are trawling again, the deckhands gut the fish and pack them in ice in the hold. That's a terrible job in rough weather. I have seen men go flying into a pile of fish and icy water. I have even known them swept overboard. Much of the time the wind is bitterly cold. The fish start to freeze solid, so it is hard to gut them. The spray that falls on the men freezes, too. All they have on their hands are rubber gloves. They gut the fish fast enough, I can tell you, in the hope that they can snatch half an hour in the warm cabin before we winch the trawl in again.'

'Where are you all this time?' 'I am on the bridge. It's heated and I am out of the weather, but there is no rest for me once we start fishing. The trawl must stay in the same depth of water, so I have to listen to my echo sounder and study my charts. I have to tell the helmsman which way to turn and shout orders down to the engine room. All the time I have

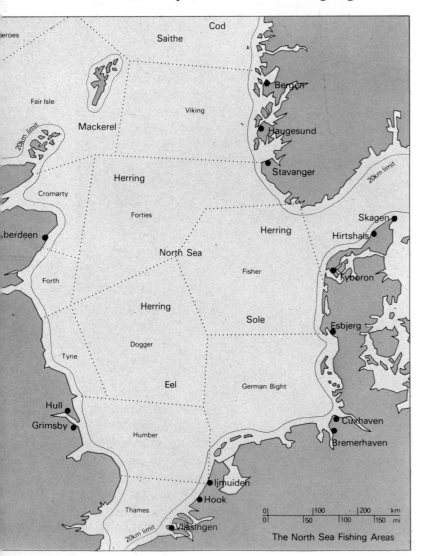

The North Sea Fishing Areas

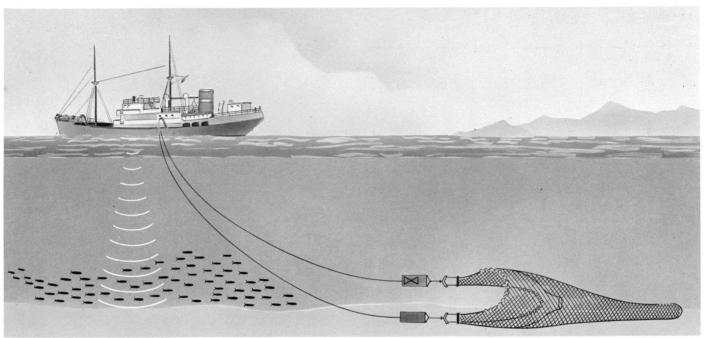
a trawler using sonar to locate fish

to watch the weather, the birds, and, especially, the other ships. If I see one of them make a good haul, we go over and join her. If we make a good haul ourselves, we try to hide it. The game is to catch all the fish you can, and rob the others. It's cut-throat competition all the time. Then I have to drive the men to their work. I find myself shouting and swearing at them more and more. I get tired, too. Some skippers let their mates take over for a few hours, but

I can't sleep while we are fishing. I eat very little, too.

'At last it's all over and we sail for home. That's a blessing, I can tell you. Sometimes I sleep for a whole day and a night. I can't count on that though, because if the weather turns bad, I have to go back to the bridge and see the ship safely through the storm. One of my friends who was a skipper was found dead in his bunk. I wasn't surprised. He was going nearly mad with worry.'

'But why is it so important to catch fish?' 'Well, for a start, I get no regular pay. The owners of the trawler give me ten per cent of the profits of each trip. The trip costs £3,000, so if we only catch fish worth that amount, I have nothing. We need to double that amount for it to be worthwhile. More important, if I didn't bring home good catches regularly, the owners would take me off this fine new ship. If I had an old tub, built before the war, I should have no chance of making a good living. I might even have to go back to being a deck hand.'

'How dangerous is fishing?' 'More dangerous than almost any other job. Quite often we have to sail in a Force 10 gale, and on land that would take the roof off your house. Ice is the big enemy though. If the weather is really cold, the spray freezes as it falls. We hack it off the decks and turn hot water hoses on it, but if we can't work fast enough, the trawler becomes top heavy, and over she goes. You don't live long if you fall into the icy waters of the Arctic Ocean: just thirty seconds, I believe.'

The Trawler Skipper

bringing the catch on board in rough seas

5 The Production Line Worker

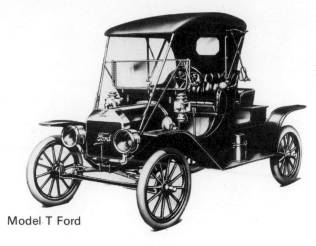
Model T Ford

Do you think you could put together all the parts that make a motor car? There are 16,000 of them! Possibly you could learn how to do this enormous puzzle, but it might take you years. However, if there are several hundred people then each one could take a different job. You might do no more than fit wheels. You could learn to do that very quickly. This method of breaking a big, complicated job into a large number of small, easy jobs is called mass production. The first man to make motor cars that way was an American called Henry Ford. Until then every car had been built by a handful of skilled craftsmen. Cars took a long time to complete and were expensive. Henry Ford's 'Model T' was so cheap that many more people could afford one, and soon car manufacturers in England were copying his way of making cars.

We will visit an imaginary car works in the 1960s to see what is happening. It belongs to the Bridge Motor Company.

We can have a good view from the catwalk. This is like a footbridge which runs the whole width of the factory. The building is enormous. Pipes snake all over the floor, there is a lot of banging and the machinery is whining. The cars stand on a huge belt,

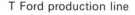
T Ford production line

about two feet from the ground, and the belt is moving steadily forward. This is the 'production line'. At the beginning, each car is just a skeleton: at the end it is finished and ready to drive away. All along the line, men are working. There are hundreds of them, each doing one job, over and over again. We can see a man fitting carpets. He turns a piece of carpet over, spreads glue on it, then puts it in place. By the time he has finished, the next car has arrived. The man does not have to hurry, but neither does he have time to waste.

It is now the tea break, so we will go and talk to Fred, one of the workers.

'What is your job, Fred?' 'I fit gearboxes. I have a supply of them beside me and when a car arrives I drop one in a hole in the engine and fix it down with a couple of bolts, I fit forty gearboxes every hour — that's three hundred and twenty a day.' *'Do you like the work?'* 'I hate it. It's so boring. How would you like to do the same thing day after day, week after week? You have to keep going, you know. If you are too slow you are carried on to the next man's patch and get all tangled up with him. Some mornings I have a headache, and would love to take it easy. The line never has a headache, though. At first I didn't think I could stick it, but I have been here for two years now.'

'Why do you do the job?' 'I do it for the money, of course. I've got a wife and a couple of children, and £17.00 a week isn't bad pay. There are plenty of men around here with no job at all. Anyway, it's better than on the building site. I was a builder's labourer before I came here. At least the factory is warm and dry.' *'What training did you have when you started?'* 'Training? What training do you need? The foreman just took me over to Bill and told him to show me what to do. Bill wasn't too pleased, but I

soon learnt the job and now I can fit a gearbox without thinking.' *'What do you think about while you are working?'* 'I don't think about anything at all. I just make my mind go a blank. It's the only way to get through the day.'

'Does the Company look after you?' 'Well, we have a canteen and a sports club, but they are only for show. We don't care about the Company, and the Company doesn't care about us. We are only numbers to them, not people. They just get all the work out of us that they can, in order to make money for themselves. If I had a problem it would be no use going to any of the bosses here. They wouldn't be interested.' *'Aren't you proud, though Fred, to see all those new shiny cars come out of the factory, and to know that you had a hand in making every one?'* 'I don't often see the finished cars as they come off the belt right down the other end, and even when I do, I can't say that I feel all that proud. I know how the lads put them together. Don't ever buy a Bridge car. You will be lucky if you find a good one. The chances are you will buy a

"Monday car", a "Friday car" or a "tea-break car", made when we're all tired or fed-up, and a whole lot of trouble will go with it.'

At the end of the shift we stand by the gate and watch the men come out. They are all in a great hurry to leave. Some walk, some have bicycles, and some have cars. Among them is Fred. He is driving a handsome, new 'Bridge Consort'.

The Production Line Worker

6 The Office Girl

As you know, difficult sums can take you a long time if you have to do them on paper. However, for hundreds of years people have been making machines to help them with their arithmetic. One of the first of these was the abacus. It is very efficient, even though it is only rows of beads on wires. Later, there were more complicated machines. In 1801, a Frenchman called Jacquard made punched cards to help weavers put patterns in their cloth, and soon other inventors were using cards like Jacquard's in arithmetic machines. People had to work such machines by hand, but in 1949 some scientists in Cambridge made the first modern electronic computer.

A computer is rather like a pocket calculator. If you are lucky enough to have one of these, you can ask it any sums you like, and it will work them out in no time at all, using electricity. Of course, full-sized computers are much more complicated. All sorts of people use them in all sorts of ways. Gunners in the army have them, as well as doctors in hospitals and astronauts. We are going to see how they have changed the work of people in offices.

We will talk to June. She is a middle-aged woman now, but back in the 1940s, when she was a girl, she started work in the general office of a small glove-making firm. There were no computers then.

'What was it like in an office in those days, June?' 'The wages were much lower then. I only earned £2.50 a week. The hours were longer too. We started at 8.30 a.m. and worked until 5.30 p.m. and had only two weeks' holiday a year. I was in a general office which meant that all of us did different jobs in the same room. I helped the chief wages clerk. It took us four days to work out the wages. We used calculating machines, of course, but we had to work them by hand, and it was a slow business. Then on Friday mornings everyone in the office helped with paying out the wages. At 9.30 a.m. the office manager and a van driver went to the local bank to collect the cash for the wages. They were for all the firm's employees: the factory workers, the office staff and the "out-workers" who made gloves in their own homes. We cleared all our papers from the desks and we each had a pile of wage slips, another of small brown packets with typed names on the outside, and bags full of pound notes, and silver and copper coins. It was very important to check the amount of money we were given and to make sure that we put the right number of notes and coins into the packets. If there was not enough money to match the wage slips, or if there was any left over at the end, then we knew we had made a mistake. We had to empty all the packets and

making up the wages in the 1940s

start again. We enjoyed this work, though, because it was a change from our other duties.'

'*Were there ever any mistakes in the wages, June?*' 'Sometimes there were and then the men and girls from the factory would come straight to the office and complain. Quite often they complained even when we hadn't made any mistake. We could check their pay slips and time cards and sort out any problems straight away. I can only remember one man who got very angry and threatened to hit the office manager.'

'*What is your work like today, June, now that you have the computer?*' 'At present I work in the wages section of a large office block in London. In this firm all the wages are worked out by the computer.' '*What does the computer do?*' 'We tell it all it needs to know about each of our employees — rate of pay, how many hours worked, tax code, and so on. We can't speak to it in the ordinary way, of course. There is a special computer language. You can't even hear it, because it is holes punched into a paper tape. The computer uses all this information to work out how much each of our employees has earned. Then it takes away tax and national insurance payments, leaving the amount the employee will actually have to spend. After the computer has finished its sums, it prints out the information on a pay slip which we send to the employees. We don't send them any actual money. Instead the wages are paid into their own bank accounts by what we call "credit transfers".'

'*Why did your firm buy a computer?*' 'To save time and money. Five years ago we had three separate departments dealing with pay, with eighty staff and twenty supervisors. When the computer was put in we only needed one office and forty people. That meant that lots of us had to change our jobs or be retrained. The supervisors all kept their jobs, of course!'

'*Is the computer efficient?*' 'Oh yes. It prepares pay slips for thousands of our workers all over the country. It only makes mistakes if we feed it the wrong information. After all, you wouldn't expect your pocket calculator to get your sums right if you gave it the wrong numbers.' '*What other differences are there between office life now and in the 1940s?*' 'Our hours are shorter than before, holidays are longer, our wages are higher and office buildings are more comfortable. But today people work in separate sections. I hardly know what is happening in other departments of the firm. I only know about wages. In some ways it was more interesting in a general office where you knew more about other people's jobs. It was fun, too, putting the wages into the pay packets. These days, of course, we should need bigger packets for the wages and I don't suppose it would be safe to bring such large amounts of money into the office. It would be too much of a temptation for criminals.'

left a modern IBM computer
top typists in a modern office

Work Section

Understand Your Work

1 The Elementary School

1 How many classes were there in Mr. Swanson's school-room? How many boys were there in each?
2 Where were the other classes?
3 What name was given to the classes?
4 What did a boy need to do to pass from one to another?
5 What was Stephen Dunton's position in the school? How old was he?
6 What were the three most important subjects? What other subjects were there?
7 What happened if the boys did well in the inspector's examination?
8 Why did Mr. Swanson make his boys work hard?
9 What sort of lesson did Stephen Dunton give?
10 How did Mr. Swanson keep discipline in his school?

2 The Boarding School

1 What was Charles Walker's school divided into?
2 What methods did the headmaster use to train the characters of his boys?
3 What privileges did prefects have?
4 What were the most important subjects in the school?
5 Which boys took science?
6 What did Charles think about school food?
7 What did he think about school games?
8 Why did he dislike being a fag?
9 Which subjects did Charles dislike?
10 Why did Charles feel his school was not giving him the education he wanted?

3 Secondary Education for All

1 What was wrong with the buildings of Brookside School in 1937?
2 What kind of school was it? At what age did most of its pupils leave?
3 For what examination did Miss Evitt prepare her children? What happened to the ones who passed?
4 What kind of school was Weston Hill?
5 What subjects were taught there?
6 Which children were in Form One Parallel?
7 Which children were in Form One?
8 What did Brookside School become in 1944? What did Weston Hill become?
9 Why was Dennis unable to go to Weston Hill?
10 What kind of schools are both Weston Hill and Brookside today?

4 The Trawler Skipper

1 Where did British trawlers go fishing in the 1960s?
2 How long does a fishing trip last? How much time is there between trips?
3 For how long does the ship trawl at a time?
4 What work does the crew do while the net is over the side? Why is it unpleasant and dangerous?
5 Why does the captain have to attend to his echo sounder and charts?
6 Why does he watch the other ships?
7 Why does he get very tired?
8 How are the skippers' wages worked out?
9 What happens to a skipper who does not bring home good catches?
10 Describe two ways in which the weather might sink a trawler.

5 The Production Line Worker

1 What is 'mass production'? Who first used mass production to make motor cars?
2 Name the moving belt in the factory on which the cars stand.
3 What kind of work are the men doing?
4 What is Fred's job?
5 Why is it boring?
6 What happens if Fred works too slowly?
7 Why does Fred work in a car factory?
8 What facilities does the Bridge Motor Company provide for its employees?
9 Why does Fred dislike the Company?
10 What does Fred say about Bridge cars? Why do you think he has bought one himself?

6 The Office Girl

1 Name some of the first calculating machines. When was the first modern electronic calculator made?
2 How long did it take to work out the wages in June's office in the 1940s?
3 What did the office staff do on Friday mornings?
4 How is information fed into a computer?
5 What calculations does the computer make?
6 How do the employees receive their wages in the 1970s?
7 Why did June's firm buy a computer?
8 When does the computer make a mistake?
9 In what ways is office work pleasanter today?
10 Why did June find her work more interesting in the 1940s?

Use Your Imagination

1 You are a pupil at Mr. Swanson's school. Say what you think of your headmaster. (1)
2 You are an inspector who has visited Mr. Swanson's school. Write a report on it. (1)
3 You are Charles Walker. Write a letter to your parents persuading them to send you to another school. (2)
4 You are the headmaster of a Victorian boarding school. Draw up a list of rules for your school. (2)
5 Write the story of Miss Evitt's life. As a girl she attended a school like Mr. Swanson's. (1, 3)
6 You are the parents of a boy or girl who has passed the scholarship examination. Explain why you are pleased. (3)
7 Your grandfather tells you education was much better in his young days. Write him a letter to persuade him he is wrong. (1, 2, 3)
8 You are on the bridge of a trawler on a fishing trip. Give a running commentary on what happens. (4)
9 How do you think life could be made more pleasant for people who make cars? (5)
10 The leader of Fred's trade union wants higher wages for the workers in the Bridge factory. He has an argument with one of the Directors. Write what they say. (5)
11 Write an advertisement for a computer explaining how it will increase office efficiency. (6)
12 You are an office worker. Your firm has installed a computer and you are now redundant. Write a letter to a newspaper, complaining about computers. (6)

Further Work

1 Find out how elementary school teachers were trained in the nineteenth century.
2 Read *Vice Versa* by F. Anstey, *Stalky and Co* by Rudyard Kipling and *Tom Brown's Schooldays* by Thomas Hughes. These are stories about boarding schools.
3 Find out how school buildings have changed since Victorian times. Quite possibly you have some old schools and some new ones in your area. If so, you can compare them.
4 Make a list of the schools in your area. Find out what kind of school each one was when it opened, and how it has changed over the years.
5 Find out what opportunities there are for Further Education in your area. For example, what courses are there at your local College of Further Education?
6 Why did Icelanders close their fishing grounds to British trawlers? What other fishing grounds have been closed to them? Write a report from the information you discover.
7 Read about methods of fishing other than trawling.
8 Talk to people who work in any of your local factories. Compare their jobs with that of a man in a car factory.
9 Find out what equipment is used in a modern office, apart from computers.
10 Think of any jobs you feel you might like to do. Find out all you can about them.

Chapter Three   Home Life and Leisure

1 The Poor Family at Home

Bath is one of the more pleasant towns in England. It has hot springs which some doctors think may help to cure rheumatism and other illnesses, so wealthy people come to the city to drink or bathe in the water. There are good hotels for them and a magnificent Pump Room. There are Roman remains, an abbey church and some splendid streets built in the eighteenth century. But not everything about Bath is pleasant. We will talk to Mr. Jardine, an inspector employed by the N.S.P.C.C.

'What is your work, Mr. Jardine?' 'I visit poor people who we think may be ill-treating their children, and try to persuade them to stop. If they will not listen to us, I have them prosecuted.' *'Surely you don't have much to do in a town like Bath?'* 'You are wrong, I'm afraid. You see, Bath is a place where rich people

come when they retire. There are army and navy officers, clergymen, gentlefolk and we even have a dowager duchess here. These people need a lot of servants, and they mainly employ women and girls. There is little work for men. Wages are low, except for skilled cabinet makers and coach builders. There are slum areas by the river, like the Dolemeads. The houses are poor, and in some winters they are flooded. The other day, I visited a house down there. The plaster was coming off the walls, the windows were broken and the roof leaked. No one had cleaned the grates for weeks, so there were ashes piled right into the room. Upstairs, they kept pigeons and the room was full of their muck. The bed was just a heap of filth, and crawling with bugs.' *'What were the children like?'* 'There was a baby lying on a heap of rags with

maggot flies buzzing all round him. He could hardly breathe because of bronchitis. There was a little boy of five in a torn shirt and an old pair of trousers. He had gangrene in a cut in his leg. There was also a girl of about eight. She had on a bodice and a bit of sacking for a skirt. All the children were covered with fleas and lice. I could hardly find a spot on the boy's back that didn't have a flea bite. The trouble with this family was that the mother was a drunkard. Things are bad when the father drinks, but if the mother drinks, there is no hope!'

Outside we find a group of boys playing, and we talk to one of them. His clothes are poor, but he is wearing shoes and is quite well fed. He must come from a better home than the one Mr. Jardine has described. He tells us his name is Frank. He is twelve years old and his father works for a builder.

'How are things at home, Frank?' 'Not too bad at the moment. Father has work now that the spring has come. I still have to do my bit to help, though.' *What do you do?'* 'I am a newsboy. I sell newspapers in the streets. I earn 2/6d (12½p) a week but I have to work hard for it. I am usually on my stand for about five hours after school and it's often ten o'clock before I've sold out. It's bitterly cold in winter and it's hard on the voice. Folk won't buy unless you shout out loud and clear. I like it best if there's been a good murder or something like that, I sell my papers quickly then.'

'What happens to your wages?' 'Mother has them, of course. Still, I can sometimes make a bit for myself. I scoop up horse muck from the streets and sell it for a farthing a bucket. (A farthing is about one-tenth of a penny.) I don't tell mother about that.'

'Do you have time to play?' 'Only on Saturdays and during the school holidays. In the summer I go off with my friends. We go into the woods, and if it's hot we undress and bathe naked in the river. That really annoys the smart young men taking their lady friends for a row. Most of the time we lark about in the streets. Sometimes we play marbles and sometimes we bowl our hoops. It makes the ladies very angry when we run into them, but it serves them right for wearing such stupid dresses. We have some good sport, especially after dark. The other night we daubed our faces with luminous paint and frightened the life out of a drunk. Once a rich old geezer who lives near here sent for the police because we were making a bit of noise outside his house. We came back later and tied a cat to his bell pull. The best part was watching the maid trying to untie the cat. We had a

a street game in East London

rare bit of good luck last winter. The Rector of Walcot went into his church and left the key in the lock. We locked the door and ran off with the key. He had to ring the bell for ages before anyone came to let him out.'

'Haven't you anywhere to play except the streets? Can't you go into the park?' 'No, the police chase us out of the Victoria Park, except when we have our school treat. Each boy has to march along carrying a cup slung over his shoulder on a strap. At the park we run races against other schools. When it's over we get a free tea of buns and lemonade. We look forward to that all the year. Boys who go to Sunday School get taken to Weston-super-Mare on the train, but I can't be bothered with Sunday School just for one day a year at the seaside.'

2 The Rich Family at Home

Mr. Walker is a solicitor. He makes a lot of money from many of the rich, retired people in Bath. They are glad to have a clever lawyer to look after their affairs so he is always busy. He is in his office at eight o'clock every morning and quite often he does not leave it, except for lunch, until eight o'clock in the evening. His wife, though, has no work to do. We will see how she spends her day.

The Walkers live in Queen's Square. It is not quite as grand as the Royal Crescent, but the houses are very elegant. They were built in the eighteenth century, and little has been done to bring them up to date. Mr. Walker sees no point in spending money to make the house easier to look after. There are plenty of poor women and girls in Bath who have to work as servants, though they earn very low wages. The main rooms are on three floors. On the ground floor is a drawing room, a dining room and Mr. Walker's study. On the other two are bedrooms. Under the roof are the attics where the servants sleep. In winter these attics are cold. In summer they are unbearably hot. Beneath the house is the basement where the servants work. There is a scullery for washing up, a larder and a kitchen. The basement is always dark

Mr. Walker

Queen's Square, Bath

and gloomy although the kitchen is always hot. The living rooms and bedrooms are always comfortable because their thick walls keep out the summer heat and in winter the servants light a fire in every room. There are thick carpets, heavy velvet curtains, expensive furniture and many ornaments and nick-nacks. To us it all looks very elaborate, cluttered and fussy. But the Walkers are proud of their fine things, which help show other people how wealthy they are.

Mrs. Walker wakes up at eight o'clock, when the maid taps on her door and brings in the breakfast tray. It may be bacon and eggs, boiled eggs, grilled kidneys or fish. Sometimes there is kedgeree, an Indian dish made from rice, eggs and fish. Next the maid makes up the fire so that it blazes merrily, and brings in a hip bath. She puts it near the fire and then fetches several cans of warm water from the kitchen. There is no bathroom in the house, but for Mrs. Walker a bath in front of the fire is very pleasant. It is not so pleasant for the maid who has to carry the water!

After bathing and dressing, Mrs. Walker goes to the drawing room and rings for the cook. Between them they decide what to serve at lunch and at dinner. Mrs. Walker has an annoying habit of changing her mind after the cook has begun to prepare a meal. For the rest of the morning Mrs. Walker hasn't very much to do. She reads a little,

plays the piano a little or does some embroidery. She usually finds the time drags until her husband comes home for lunch.

After lunch, Mrs. Walker begins what is for her the serious business of the day. She makes her 'calls', and goes round to see her friends and neighbours. She takes a little ivory case with her in which she keeps her visiting cards. She might leave a card at a house to say thank you for a dinner party, or perhaps to say she was sorry to hear someone was ill. Mrs. Walker bends one corner of each card to show she has called in person. Now and then, she may ask to see the lady of the house. Again, she will leave a card if the maid says, 'Not at home.' When she has paid all her calls, she returns home, anxious to see if anyone important has left a card for her.

On many afternoons Mrs. Walker attends an 'at home' and sometimes she gives one herself. These are elegant little afternoon parties. The maid announces each visitor by name and they all sit in the drawing room, drinking tea and eating very thin slices of bread and butter and tiny cakes. Perhaps someone will play the piano to entertain them.

In the early evening Mrs. Walker sees her children for half an hour. She finds them noisy and tiresome, so she is glad when the nurse takes them away. She now dresses for dinner, the most important event of the day. First she puts on a cotton shift, and then a corset. The idea of the corset is to hold her waist in and give her an 'hour-glass' figure. Mrs. Walker holds the back of a chair while the housemaid and tweeny, or junior maid, pull the corset laces as tight as they can. Next comes the bustle (a bone framework which makes the dress stick out at the back). On top of the bustle comes a petticoat and then comes the dress itself, a beautiful pink silk one trimmed with white lace.

For dinner there are a large number of French dishes, which are really too complicated for the cook to make properly. When it is over the family and the guests go into the drawing room where they drink coffee, play cards and gossip, until it is time for bed.

3 Domestic Servants

In the 1890s, over a million women and girls worked as domestic servants. A rich nobleman might employ as many as three hundred servants, but even a solicitor, like Mr. Walker, had four. They were a nurse, a housemaid, a cook and a tweeny. The nurse looked after the children. The housemaid saw that the house was clean and tidy, as well as doing other jobs such as receiving callers and helping her mistress to dress. The cook prepared all the meals. The tweeny, or between maid, helped the housemaid in the morning and the cook in the afternoon. We will talk to the tweeny, who is called Eliza.

'Where do you come from, Eliza?' 'I was born in Gurney Slade, about fifteen miles away.' *'How did you become a servant?'* 'There were eight children in our

family and father thought it would be a good idea for me to go into service. There was precious little else to do. When I was eleven I started as a slavey with a shopkeeper at Gurney Slade.' *'What is a slavey?'* 'I was the only servant they had, so I did all the work — the fires, the cleaning, the washing up, looking after the children and the washing and ironing. The only thing the mistress did was the cooking, and a fine mess she used to leave for me to clear up! Then the rector heard that Mr. Walker wanted a tweeny, so I came to work in Bath.' *'Are things better for you now?'* 'Not a lot. I still have to get up at six in the morning, though I can usually go to bed by ten. It used to be midnight more often than not.'

'What work do you have to do?' 'I am first up in the morning. I have to creep down, making sure I don't wake anybody, and then I light the range. First of all I have to clean out the ashes and polish the top of the stove until it shines. When the kettle boils I take Jane the cook and Ellen the housemaid a cup of tea. When Ellen gets up I help her lay breakfast and take the mistress her breakfast in bed. I have to go round and make sure there is a good fire in every room. The family doesn't like to be cold. I also have to take them their hot water. I am up and down stairs all the time it seems, carrying heavy buckets. The master once lifted my bucket of coal and said it must weigh about thirty pounds, but he didn't offer to carry it for me.

'After the family has dressed we do the bedrooms. I have to do the dirty jobs, of course. I see to the fires and I empty the chamber pots. They have to be rinsed and wiped out. Sometimes that makes me feel sick. To clean the carpets, I scatter tea leaves everywhere and then brush them up. That picks up the dust you see. Making beds is a game! Each one has three mattresses. There is a straw one at the bottom which we only turn once a week. Next there is a wool one that we turn every day. Lastly, there is the feather one which we have to shake until it's all puffed up. There are the living rooms as well, of course — grates, carpets and the dusting. The floors have to be spotless, even under carpets. The missus once hid a shilling under a carpet, just to see if we cleaned underneath and if we were honest.

'In the afternoon I have to help the cook. There is the washing up from lunch, and there are all the vegetables to prepare for the evening meal. Cook is old and bad-tempered and often has a drop too much to drink. I have to make the fire roar away so the kitchen gets as hot as a furnace. It's dreadful in summer. Ellen usually waits at table, but if the family has friends to dinner I help her. I hate that. They all sit there in their finery, talking posh. I feel scared I am going to drop something. Once, someone said something which made me giggle and I couldn't stop. The missus was furious. We aren't supposed to listen to the conversation. She wouldn't hear my excuses. "I allow no answers," she said.

'After dinner there is a mountain of washing up – everything from delicate wine glasses to great sticky copper pans. I once counted sixty knives and forks, forty spoons and a hundred plates. It was well after midnight before I finished all that.'

'Do you ever leave the house?' 'Only to wash the doorstep and as I'm from the country I do miss the fields and woods. This house is like a prison. I have a half day on Sunday, but they make me go to church. Once a month I have a full day, and can go home to see my family – that's if missus doesn't find me a job so that I miss my train.'

'How much do you earn for all that work?' 'I get ten pounds a year and have to buy my uniform out of that.' *'Do you have any boyfriends?'* 'Followers, do you mean? I'm no dolly mop, but there is a boy back home who rather likes me. He walked all the way to Bath to see me, but I had to send him away at once. If the family knew I had a follower, they would sack me on the spot.'

4 Washday

Mr. and Mrs. Cox and their eight children live on the outskirts of Bath. Mr. Cox owns a lock-up shop in the centre of town and the family are comfortably off. They are not rich, but they can afford to have someone to help Mrs. Cox with the housework. Mrs. Parsons comes in from a nearby village every Monday. Both women dislike Mondays and even the Cox children are glad when Monday is over. We will ask Lily, one of the daughters, why she does not like Mondays.

'None of us likes Monday because it's washday and that means a scrappy cold lunch of leftovers and nothing very nice for tea and supper either. Mother is so busy all day that she doesn't have time to bother with cooking. By the evening she is always tired and cross. One of us is usually in trouble before bedtime. You can hardly get inside the kitchen on Monday evening anyway, because it is always full of drying clothes and piles of ironing.'

Now let us see what Mrs. Cox herself thinks about Monday. *'Please tell us about washday, Mrs. Cox.'* 'First of all, before my husband leaves to open the shop, he lights the fire under the boiler. By the time Mrs. Parsons arrives to help me the water is very hot. The boiler uses quite a lot of coal but I boil all my whites in the copper and get them really clean, the way I like them. When they are finished we lift them out with a boiler stick and put them into baths of water: a bath of rinsing water, one of starch and then a bowl of blue. When the clothes have been through the baths we lift them out for mangling.' *'How do you fill the boiler and the baths with water, Mrs. Cox?'* 'I'm lucky because there is a tap and a low sink in the corner of the wash-house. We fill up with buckets of water from the tap and empty them into the sink. It's sometimes difficult to get every drop of dirty water out of the boiler, but I have a special little round bowl with a wooden handle. It's very useful for scooping out the last drops of water.' *'Do you put all your clothes into the boiler, Mrs. Cox?'* 'Dear me, no, I certainly don't boil my coloured things. I wash those in a dolly tub. First of all I pound away at the washing with a dolly, which is rather like a three-legged stool with a tall handle in the middle. I rub the really dirty clothes on my rubbing board with some good strong

yellow soap.' *'Do you use soap powder, Mrs. Cox?'* 'What's soap powder? All I need is soap, soda and lots of elbow grease. The soda is a bit hard on the hands and Mrs. Parsons and I usually have raw, red hands by Monday evening. We have to put soda in the water to make the soap lather well.'

'What happens next?' 'We put the clothes through the mangle, which is the hardest work of all. I have a large mangle with heavy beech rollers. The handle is hard to turn. Luckily, Mrs. Parsons is strong. I can only just manage it and when the children are at home in the holidays it takes two of them to turn the handle while I guide the sheets through the rollers. The water drains straight into the sink which is just above floor level. A heavy mangle is best because it squeezes most of the water out of the washing and then it does not take too long to dry. As I have a garden, I can dry my washing easily when the weather is fine, but in bad weather it is often hanging on clothes horses around the kitchen stove for days.'

'What do you do when the clothes are dry?' 'Well, I mustn't let some of the things get too dry or they are very hard to iron. It usually takes me most of Tuesday to finish ironing which I do on my big wooden table in the kitchen. It's hard work and it gets very hot because there has to be a good fire in the stove to heat up the irons. I have two big cast iron ones and while I am using one iron, the other is re-heating on the trivet in front of the fire. I also have a polishing iron which I use for my husband's stiff collars. Ironing shirts is bad enough, but it takes ages to do my daughters' cotton petticoats and long frilly drawers because there is so much material in them.'

As we have learnt from the Cox family, washing and ironing in Victorian times meant hours of

drudgery. As you know from your own homes, it is different today. What helped to bring about this change? Mrs. Cox's only source of power was coal, but during the twentieth century another important source of power was developed – electricity. At first there were lots of separate electricity companies and they were not always well organized. Then, between 1926 and 1935, workmen were busy all over the country building the huge pylons that can be seen everywhere. They carry a network of cables that we call the National Grid. This joins together all the different power stations, so that each one is helping to supply the whole country with electricity. The National Grid is the responsibility of the Central Electricity Generating Board and the country is divided into twelve areas, each with its own board.

Electricity has brought many changes into people's lives. It has certainly altered washday. In the 1930s Mrs. Cox's young daughter Lily was the first person in her road to own an electric washboiler.

Compared with today's washing machines it was a very simple affair. All the mangling still had to be done by hand. But the neighbours thought Lily was very lucky. 'You won't know yourself now,' they said.

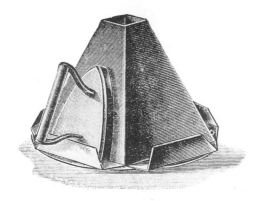

The Music Hall

6 Radio and Cinema

In 1896 an Italian called Marconi discovered how to send Morse code messages through the air. People were already sending such messages, but along telegraph cables. Thanks to Marconi they could manage without the cables, so they called his invention 'wireless telegraphy'. It was especially useful to ships.

Then, on Christmas Eve, 1906, the wireless operators on ships near the coast of America were amazed. Their sets should only have sent them the dots and dashes of the Morse code, but they were talking and playing music! It was one of the world's first radio broadcasts.

In Britain, the British Broadcasting Company started regular programmes in 1922 and four years later two million families owned wireless sets or 'radios' as some called them. The mother of one of these families will tell us about it.

'The radio is wonderful entertainment, of course. We have the Children's Hour, which keeps the little ones quiet for a while. My older boy laughs at it. "It's kids' stuff," he says, "with all those soppy uncles and aunties." What he likes is "Radio Dance Band". I like classical music myself. We could never go to a concert because we are so far from town, but now we have the concerts in our own home. My husband is interested in feature programmes which are often very realistic because they use music and sound

a live broadcast in 1923

effects. I wish they would broadcast in the mornings as well. Some nice music would cheer up the housework.'

'Has the radio given you any problems?' 'Well, sometimes I have trouble getting the children to bed. I find, too, that some of our neighbours drop in more often than they used to. They can't afford their own radios, so they come and listen to ours. They expect tea and biscuits as well!' *'Do you find the radio keeps your family at home?'* 'I suppose the children spend less time in the streets, but I'm afraid it would take more than the wireless to keep my husband out of the Red Lion on a Saturday night.'

We will now ask a teacher about school broadcasts. 'A waste of time. They are never relevant to our work. How can a machine replace a teacher? I would never have a wireless in my house, let alone in my school. As for my pupils, they just listen to "the voice" these days and never think for themselves. It's a bad influence, too. I caught a boy hammering out jazz on the school piano the other day, and two girls dancing the Charleston. What really worries me, though, is this man Baird who has invented television. If people have the confounded cinema in their homes it will be the ruin of everything we do in school.'

While wireless sets became a part of life in the home, the cinema became the most popular form of public entertainment. The very first film performance in England was in 1896. Soon films were being shown all over the country. For the first time people outside London were able to see important events, such as the funeral of Queen Victoria and the Coronation of Edward VII.

The early films, of course, had no sound at all. The words the actors spoke were printed on cards which came up on the screen every few seconds. A pianist played music to suit the action of the film — fast exciting music for fights and chases and soft, sweet music for love scenes. The first film to use sound was *The Jazz Singer* in 1927, in which Al Jolson sang, but did not speak. The following year brought the first talking film.

The new 'talkies' were a great success. Almost every small town had one cinema, and there were a

number to choose from in the larger towns. Probably the cinema was most popular during the 1930s and the early 1940s. The films and stars from Hollywood were known and loved all over the world. We will visit a small town in the West of England to talk to a shop assistant called Shirley.

'*How often do you go to the pictures, Shirley?*' 'There are two separate programmes at the Palladium every week, so I always go on Monday evenings. On Saturday night my boyfriend takes me to the late performance. Sometimes we go to Bristol on Sundays if there is a very good film showing. It's not very expensive when you think of how much we enjoy the films – only 1/6d (7½p) for the ordinary seats and 3/– (15p) for the best ones. Anyway, there's nothing else to do here, particularly in the winter.'

'*What kind of films do you enjoy?*' 'Well, I like almost all kinds really, but I particularly enjoy love stories and musicals, although my boyfriend's favourites are the Westerns. We enjoy funny films too. Laurel and Hardy always make me laugh. My favourite stars, are Joan Crawford and Clark Gable. I wrote to Hollywood once and they sent me their autographs. I'd queue all day to see any film that starred either of them. Life would be miserable without the cinema, I think. Going to the pictures is a really good night out and it's something to look forward to when I'm at work.'

Work Section

Understand Your Work

1 The Poor Family at Home
1 What is the work of an N.S.P.C.C. inspector?
2 Why are wages low in Bath?
3 What was wrong with the house Mr. Jardine described?
4 How were the children suffering from their mother's neglect?
5 Why was she a bad mother?
6 How does Frank earn money?
7 Who takes his wages?
8 Where do Frank and his friends go to enjoy themselves?
9 In what ways are the boys a nuisance?
10 What entertainment is organized for poor children?

2 The Rich Family at Home
1 Why have the Walkers not modernized their home?
2 What rooms are there on each floor of the house?
3 How are the living rooms furnished?
4 Where does Mrs. Walker have her breakfast, and her bath?
5 How does Mrs. Walker spend her morning?
6 How does she spend her afternoon?
7 What is an 'at home'?
8 How long does Mrs. Walker spend with her children?
9 What clothes does Mrs. Walker wear for dinner?
10 What kind of food is served for dinner?

3 Domestic Servants
1 How many women and girls were domestic servants in the 1880s?
2 How many servants might a nobleman have?
3 What servants did the Walkers have? Explain what each one had to do.
4 Why did Eliza become a servant?
5 What is a 'slavey'?
6 How many hours does Eliza work in a day?
7 Make a list of the jobs she does.
8 How much free time does Eliza have?
9 How much money does she earn?
10 What would happen if her employer discovered she had a boyfriend?

4 Washday
1 Which day of the week is washday?
2 Why do Mrs. Cox's children dislike washday?
3 Make a list of all the equipment Mrs. Cox needs for washing. Say what each item is used for.
4 A modern housewife uses soap powder or detergent. What does Mrs. Cox use?
5 How are the clothes dried?
6 How does Mrs. Cox do her ironing?
7 Why does it take such a long time?
8 What is the National Grid? When was it set up?
9 Who is responsible for the National Grid?
10 How did electricity help Mrs. Cox's daughter, Lily?

5 Sundays and Holidays
1 How did Mr. Fussell's sons get ready for church?
2 What does the family do after church?
3 How do the boys spend Sunday afternoon and evening?
4 How can the Fussell's enjoy themselves out of doors, near home?
5 What can they do in Bristol?
6 Which circus visits Bath?
7 What sort of play is staged at the theatre in Bath?
8 Where do the Fussells have to sit in the theatre?
9 Which music hall artist did the Fussells see in Bristol?
10 Why did Mrs. Fussell pretend she did not enjoy the performance?

6 Radio and Cinema
1 Who invented wireless telegraphy? When?
2 When did the B.B.C. start regular radio broadcasts?
3 What sort of programmes were they?
4 What problems might the radio cause?
5 Why did some people object to the radio?
6 When was the first film performance in England?
7 How did the early films make up for not having sound?
8 When was the first talking film shown?
9 What differences did the cinema make to the lives of people living in a small town in the 1930s?
10 Name some of the film stars of those days.

Use Your Imagination

1 You are a wealthy citizen in Bath. Write a letter to the local newspaper complaining about the behaviour of children in the streets. (1)
2 An N.S.P.C.C. inspector tries to persuade a woman who is neglecting her children to take better care of them. Write what he says. (1)
3 Write a page from Mrs. Walker's diary, describing a typical day. (2)
4 You are Mrs. Walker's tweeny, Eliza. Write a letter to a friend saying what you think of your mistress. (2, 3)
5 Write a list of instructions that Mrs. Walker might have drawn up for her tweeny. (3)
6 Mrs. Cox and Mrs. Parsons talk as they do the Monday wash. Write out their conversation. Nearly everything they say is about the washing, e.g. they ask each other for help, or wonder if there is enough sun to dry the clothes. (4)
7 Write an advertisement for one of the earliest electric wash boilers. (How is it going to make washday easier?) (4)
8 Suppose Mr. Fussell could be brought back to life today. What do you think he would say about the way you spend your weekends? (5)
9 A bank holiday is just over. Mrs. Fussell tells a friend how her family spent it. Write what she says. (5)
10 It is 1930. Two people have an argument: one is in favour of the radio and the cinema; the other is against them. Describe their argument. (6)
11 It is 1922. Your father has bought one of the first radio sets. Write a letter to a friend and tell him or her all about it. (6)
12 In what ways has life become easier and more pleasant for ordinary people in the last hundred years? (All sections)

Further Work

1 Make a list of the things that are done today to try and prevent the evils mentioned in the first section of this chapter.
2 Find examples of Victorian furniture and ornaments. Look in antique shops and museums. You may have some Victorian things in your own home.
3 Look for pictures of Victorian ladies and gentlemen, and make a study of their costume.
4 Find out about male servants, e.g. butlers and valets.
5 Very few people are servants today. In fact, their numbers have been falling ever since the First World War. Try to find out why.
6 Make a list of all the improvements that electricity has brought to our homes.
7 Find out more about the history of electricity supply.
8 Read about the history of the gas industry.
9 Read more about the history of the music hall, especially the life of Marie Lloyd.
10 Find out about the early days of television.

Chapter Four   The Countryside

1 The Farm Worker and his Family

Today we will visit Gurney Slade, a small village on the Mendip Hills fifteen miles south of Bath. We will travel by the Somerset and Dorset Railway – the S. & D. Some people call it the 'Slow and Dirty', but girls from the village who work in Bath are very glad it is there, because otherwise they could not go home. The same railway takes wealthy Bath families to Bournemouth for their holidays. The village farmers are also grateful for the railway because it carries their milk to Bath. Their grandfathers had been unable to send fresh milk to market so they had to turn all the milk into cheese and butter.

We will leave the train at Binegar station and walk a mile to the home of the Woodget family. The lane has a surface of loose stones and is damp and muddy. In one place the hedges are so tall and over-hang the lane so much that it is like walking through a tunnel. Near the village there are stone walls, and the wide grass verges are yellow with primroses. It is peaceful and beautiful.

The Woodgets live in a tiny cottage. There is one room downstairs which has a stone floor. It is only twelve feet square and the ceiling is so low that we can touch it. The stairs are not much better than a

ladder. They lead to a small bedroom where the parents and four children all sleep together. It is not surprising that the family are pleased because Eliza, one of their daughters, has left home to work in service in Bath. She is the tweeny you met in Chapter Three.

Mrs. Woodget cooks over the living room fire. There is a hook for roasting joints. It hangs down from the chimney and has a clockwork device that makes it turn. There is a kind of tin oven for baking which has to stand open in front of the fire. There is also an iron plate with a number of little hooks. This is for roasting sparrows. The most important thing though, is a large iron pot in which a whole supper can be cooked. There may be bacon, beans, potatoes and roly-poly pudding. Mrs. Woodget puts each type of food into a separate net and drops it into the pot at a different time. She uses the same pot to boil the clothes on washday.

Mrs. Woodget is a tall strong woman wearing a long dress that reaches to her ankles. The dress is coarse and plain, but her apron is sparkling white. Her hands are brown and hard but her face is not at all sunburnt. She spends many hours outside but she is always careful to wear her bonnet. All the women think that a sun tan would spoil their looks.

'What do you do during the day, Mrs. Woodget?' 'I am very busy looking after my home and my family. I get up at half past five and make breakfast and dinner for my husband and oldest boy. I tie the food up in handkerchiefs. Sometimes the boy gives me a bit of trouble. His boots dry out, you see, and the leather gets very hard. He doesn't want to put them on because they hurt his feet. He goes off to work in the end and I have a bit of bread and lard for break-fast. Then it's time to see the younger children off to school. I spend the morning fetching water from the pump in the village and cleaning the house. In the afternoons I garden or have a couple of hours with my friends drinking a cup of tea. Then I must make up my fire and cook supper for the family.'

'How much housekeeping money do you have?' 'My husband earns a gold half-sovereign a week. That's ten shillings (50p). I give him back one shilling for pocket money. My boy, George, earns two shillings. I have to pay the rent of the cottage which is one shilling and sixpence (7½p) a week. Sometimes I buy some biscuits and an orange or two, but mainly I buy tea, sugar, cheese and bread – especially bread.' 'Is that all you live on?' 'Goodness no. We have a big allotment and that grows us enough potatoes to last us the year, and some oats as well. Then there is the garden. That gives us cabbages, celery, onions, beans, cauliflowers, and fruit too in the summer. And where do ·you think that comes from?' (Mrs. Woodget points to some bacon hanging on the wall.) 'Better than any picture, isn't it? We fatten and kill a pig every year. We never go hungry, but clothes worry me. My husband earns a bit extra at hay making time. I work on the farm then for a few weeks too. Still, that doesn't pay for much more than our boots. It's lucky our girl is in service with a good family. They let her have their cast-offs to send us. The vicar's wife helps, too. She runs some charities and often gives me a bit of cloth when one of the children needs a dress.'

Mr. Woodget is a large, brawny man. He is wearing heavy boots, corduroy trousers and a coarse, cotton jacket, but no shirt. As it is Sunday, he is going to have a shave, but he hasn't done that yet, so his face is covered in stubble. He is still quite young and is very strong. He has never known a day's illness, but one day he will suffer for the life he is spending outside in all kinds of weather. Most of the old men in the village are crippled with rheumatism.

'Tell us about your work, Mr. Woodget.' 'I work on Mr. Dando's farm. There are the cows to be milked every day, but the rest of the work depends on the season. Hay making is the busiest time, of course. We have a reaper to cut the grass, but Mr. Dando doesn't have a tedder, so we have to turn the hay with pitchforks. It's an anxious time watching the weather. Too much rain washes the goodness out of the hay, and turns it mouldy. As soon as it's dry we have to get it into the yard and stack it. The waggons go to and from the fields from dawn until dark. We enjoy the hay harvest, though. Mr. Dando gives us plenty of cider to help us keep working. That's better than the cold tea my wife gives me the rest of the year.' 'What about the corn harvest?' 'Farmers round here don't grow a lot of corn. They used to in the old days, my father told me, but now we just have a few acres of oats and barley for cattle feed.'

1 The Farm Worker and his Family

'*Your work must need a lot of strength, Mr. Woodget?*' 'Strength, yes, but it needs skill too. You see that little silver cup? I won that for ploughing. I drive a straighter furrow than anyone else in these parts. How would you get on with thatching a rick, do you think? My ricks are thatched as neat and snug as any house. Did you see that hedge as you came up the lane? I cut and laid that this winter. There's no townsman born could ever do a job like that.' '*Does the weather interfere much with your work?*' 'We have to stop in very heavy rain, but otherwise I just fling a sack over my shoulders and carry on. Mr. Dando says "Plough when the north-east wind is in the air. That's what kills the germ in the soil." He doesn't seem to worry about killing his ploughman as well!'

Soon, George Woodget comes home. He is twelve but is small for his age. He is wearing a shirt with no collar, a coat several sizes too big with no buttons,

harvest-time

and torn, baggy trousers. They are so stiff with meal and mud that they look as if they would stand up on their own. He wears a shapeless hat with a wide, tattered brim that falls over his eyes. He has no socks, and on his feet are huge boots, caked with mud. It is now twelve o'clock and he has already been working for six hours but as it is Sunday he has finished for the day. He has a job on a dairy farm and cows need milking and feeding every day. He tells us about his work during the week.

'I have to be at the farm by six o'clock. First, I clean out the stable and water the horses. Next, I go into the cow-shed to help with the milking. Mr. Gough, the farmer, has thirty cows, but several of us work together and we usually finish by half of eight o'clock (7.30). Then I can snatch a few minutes for breakfast. Mother gives me bread and cold tea. After breakfast I drive the cows to the fields, and then come back and help clean out the cow-shed. We pile the dung in the yard. When it is rotten we load it in a cart and take it to the fields. One of the men throws it out of the cart, while I lead the horse. I do all sorts of other jobs too. I have to carry hay and clean straw to the cow-house and stable, chop sticks for firewood, and collect the eggs from the hen-house.

When we have calves, Mr. Gough boils up meal and I feed it to them. I spilt a whole lot down my trousers today and got a beating. The cows need milking again in the evening, of course. Mr. Gough gives me an hour for dinner. I usually go up in the hay loft. It's bread and cold tea again, but I generally have a bit of cheese as well – that's if I didn't eat it for breakfast. Usually, mother gives me a bit of pudding from last night's supper.

'After dinner, I have to work until nightfall, and walk home in the dark. I don't like that very much. Sometimes gypsies camp by the lane and there are ghosts in the woods. I have to pass Mother Giddings's cottage, too. She's a witch. It's good to get home on a winter's night, I can tell you. Mother always has a hot meal for us, even if it's only potatoes and cabbage.'

'*How do you enjoy yourself, George?*' 'I don't have much time for playing. I can't even have a lark with the two other boys at the farm. Mr. Gough won't let us work together. He says "A boy is a boy: two boys are half a boy: three boys are no boy at all." '

left threshing wheat by steam power

69

2 The Farmer

It is time to visit George Woodget's employer, Mr. Gough. His house is set near the road and has a hedge of neatly clipped yew. It is no use knocking on the handsome front door because that is only opened for weddings and funerals. Instead, we will go round to the back of the house and into the kitchen.

The kitchen has a floor made from flagstones. It is uneven and cold, but perfectly clean. There is one small window with the farmer's rocking chair beside it, so that he can see to read his newspaper. The fireplace is huge, and has chimney corners with little stools in them. There is a wooden settle (a kind of bench), a deal table well worn with scrubbing, and some Windsor chairs.

There is a parlour, too, which has a carpet, velvet curtains, wallpaper, a settee and some easy chairs. But the parlour is used as seldom as the front door, and for the same reasons. All the life of the house takes place in the kitchen. A hundred years before the farmer's wife fed the workers there. The cowman, carter and the labourers used to clump in, wearing their heavy, muddy boots, and have huge meals of bread, cheese, bacon and cider. That has not happened for a long time and now the men eat at

home or, during the day, out in the fields. Mr. and Mrs. Gough eat and live in their kitchen and also entertain friends there.

Beside the kitchen is a scullery. Here, Mrs. Gough and her maid prepare the food and do the washing up. It is a low, dark room. The sink is old and worn. There is one great luxury though. The pump is inside the room. The maid still has to pump water, but at least she does not have to go outside. This maid is unhappy. She does not like Mrs. Gough, and still less does she like being 'in service' in a farm. She hopes that she will soon find a place in a smart house in Wells, or even in Bath.

The farmers in the district visit each other quite often during the winter evenings. They sit round the kitchen table and play cards by the light of an oil lamp. To make it more interesting they gamble, but only with pennies or halfpennies. No more than a few shillings change hands during the evening. They drink big mugs of cider, and in cold weather they sometimes dip a red-hot poker into the cider to warm it. Mrs. Gough keeps the fire blazing, so it is hard to go out into the cold at the end of the evening. Most people travel by dog-cart. They button their overcoats and wrap rugs round their knees because they have to sit up in the biting wind, the rain or the snow. The horse clip-clops through the lonely lanes, and the only light comes from two feeble lanterns flickering on either side of the cart. But there is not much danger, because the horse knows every bend and pot-hole in the road. It is not often that a farmer is so drunk that he does not know where he is going, but, if by any chance he is, then he can count on his horse to take him home.

Most of the time people have to make their own amusements, but once a year there is a sheep fair at Priddy, and a horse fair at Binegar. Farmers buy and sell animals at the fairs, but there are side-shows as well. Friends from miles around meet to gossip and drink together, and in the evening there is dancing on the village green. Priddy is a few miles away, but Binegar is the next village. The horse fair brings worries as well as pleasures. Gypsies and tinkers as well as all sorts of ruffians come, and there is always a chance that a drunken gang may attack a lonely

farmhouse. Mr. Gough usually has some gold coins in the house, kept in a big oak chest, so he is afraid his money might be stolen. He also has a big, old sword in the chest. On the night of Binegar Fair, he takes it out, and puts it on top of the chest. It is rusty with age, and not at all sharp, but he feels safer when he has it ready. Luckily, he has never had to use it.

On Sunday Mr. and Mrs. Gough, with their two grown-up sons, walk across the fields to church. Mrs. Gough wears a large bonnet, a shawl, and a long, flower-patterned skirt with a bustle. Bustles are now out of fashion in the towns, but the country women still think they are smart. The men wear black suits, in place of their week-day jackets, breeches and gaiters. Mr. Gough has a pew near the front of the church. He sits close behind the squire. Most of the other farmers are behind him, and the tradespeople like the grocer and the innkeeper are behind the farmers. The few labourers who come sit right at the back of the church. Mr. Gough is a churchwarden. More than that, he has just given a lot of money to pay for new pews. He feels his neighbours should be grateful. In fact they are rather jealous and say the new pews are not nearly as comfortable as the old ones.

The Farmer

Now let us see what is behind the farmhouse. It has been raining and the farmyard is a sea of mud. Around the yard are the buildings. The most important is the cow stall, with room for thirty cows. Above it is a hay loft, with trapdoors, so that the hay can be tossed into the mangers down below. The farm cat lives in the hay loft with her four kittens. Then there are stables for the horses, and sheds for the carts as well as for Mr. Gough's mowing machine. The only other piece of modern equipment is the cream separator. One of the women pours milk in at the top, while another turns a handle. Cream then comes out of one spout and skimmed milk from another. The cream goes to make butter, and the skimmed milk is fed to the pigs. The wives of the farm workers can have a jug of skimmed milk for a penny, but they do not usually bother with it. Beyond the yard is a paddock with several large horses. They are fine animals and we stop to admire them. Last of all, we visit the dairy which is cool and spotlessly clean. This is Mrs. Gough's department and she is pleased to show us round.

'We churn a little butter, but mainly we make cheese. In this part of Somerset it is Cheddar, of course. First we heat the milk until it is warm. We used to do that by guesswork, but I have a thermometer now. Then we put in rennet, if you know what that is. Well, whenever we kill a young calf, we are careful to keep the stomach because inside there is some half-digested milk, all curdled. That's rennet. If you put a couple of spoonfuls into twelve gallons of warm milk, it soon divides it into curds and whey.' *'Do you mean it goes sour?'* 'It looks rather like that. Next we have to separate off the whey, break up the curd and put it in the press. We press it several times to squeeze out all the whey, and make the cheese nice and firm. Then the cheeses must stay for a while on the shelves to cure. We have to turn and wipe them every day. It's hard work in a dairy. When my mother was an old lady her hands used to shake all the time, so that she couldn't even hold a teacup. The doctor said that was because she worked too hard in her dairy when she was younger.'

We go back into the kitchen and Mr. Gough talks about his farm. *'You seem to be earning a good living,*

making cheese

Mr. Gough.' 'I'm not doing too badly, thank you. But times are not as good as they were. Back in the 1860s farmers lived like gentlemen. A lot has happened since then. There's all this wheat they bring in from America. Our farmers can't grow it at double the price. They bring frozen lambs in from New Zealand and beef from South America. It's nothing like the home-grown meat, but it's dirt cheap.' *'But you don't produce wheat or meat.'* 'That's right. Somerset farmers used to think themselves unlucky because it is too wet here for corn or beef cattle. We have always produced milk. Now we are in luck, because milk is the one thing they can't bring in from abroad.' *'Do you make a lot of cheese?'* 'A fair bit, but most of my milk is sold fresh. We take the churns down to Binegar station, first thing in the morning. Some goes north to Bath, some goes south to Bournemouth. All of it reaches the customers the same day. I don't know how we would manage without the railway.'

'Don't you grow any crops at all, Mr. Gough?' 'Only a few oats and a bit of barley. None of it leaves the farm because I use it all as cattle feed. But don't you forget that grass is a crop. I have to chain harrow it, and manure it to make it grow. Making hay is a big job, too.' *'You don't have much machinery.'* 'I have a

a modern demonstration of threshing by steam power

his leg, so he doesn't feel any pain and walks evenly. It will be days before the customer sees there is something wrong. I don't do that sort of thing. I only stooped to dishonesty once and that was when I was a young man. My father sent me to London to buy some horses and I had to put them in a field with lots of others. In the morning all of mine had gone. I knew the old man would half-kill me, so I took someone else's horses and got away as fast as I could. I was frightened, I can tell you. I would have spent a long time in prison if I had been caught.'

horses at work on the land

mowing machine, and my men say I should buy a tedder. I say they can turn the hay just as well with a pitch-fork. A dairy farmer doesn't need much machinery. Why should I buy expensive machines when the men will work for ten shillings a week?'

'*Don't you think you should pay your men more?*' 'Certainly not! How would they spend the money? They all have houses and some of my best workers live in them rent-free. I never knew one of them go hungry. What use would fancy food be to them? A man does better on bread and bacon than on beef steaks and pies. To work hard you must live hard. They all look happy enough when each has his golden half-sovereign on pay-day.' '*But how do you manage to thresh your oats and barley?*' 'A contractor comes round with a threshing machine and a steam engine. He can finish my lot easily in a day.' '*You seem to have a lot of horses, Mr. Gough.*' 'Yes, that's a useful sideline of mine. I breed shire horses.'

Mr. Gough proudly shows us some cups he has won at the Bath and West Show. But Mrs. Gough says her husband frightens the life out of her because whenever he sees some horses in a field, he must go and look at them. He lifts their hooves, looks in their mouths, then cracks his whip to see how they gallop. She is afraid he will be kicked to death one day.

'*Horse dealers have a bad name, don't they, Mr. Gough?*' 'Well they do get up to all sorts of dodges. For instance, if a horse limps you can cut a nerve in

3 The Village Wheelwright

Now let's see what happens in the village wheelwright's shop. We will talk to one of the men who works there. *'What kinds of things do you make, Mr. Maggs?'* 'We make anything the farmers want, from milking stools which cost them sixpence (2½p) to four-wheeled waggons worth £50.' *'It must be skilled work.'* 'It is indeed. I had to do a seven-year apprenticeship, and even then it was a long time before I was any good at my trade. You need a lot of skill and strength to use the tools, and you need to know about wood. The best made wheel will fall apart in no time if you put just one bad bit of wood in it.'

'How do you make a wheel?' 'We call the piece in the middle the stock. I turn that on the lathe so that it's nice and round. Then I cut holes in it with my chisel for the spokes. The stock is made of elm wood,

but the spokes must be heart of oak. I chop them roughly to shape with an axe, just as you do firewood. Next, I make each one smooth with a plane and a spoke shave. I put one end against the bench and hold the other with my stomach.' Mr. Maggs opens his shirt and shows us a hard patch of skin, where he has pressed against hundreds of spokes. 'The spokes have to fit tightly in the stock — so tightly that I have to drive them in with a sledge-hammer. I can't hit them just anyhow, though. They have to go in at just the right angle. The rim of the wheel is made of felloes.' (Mr. Maggs pronounces this 'fellees.') 'These are separate curved pieces of wood. Each one forms part of a circle. I chop them into shape with my axe, and then one of the boys planes them smooth. Each felloe takes two spokes, so I have to drill two holes in

hammer. The wheel makes noises like whips cracking.

The owner of the business, Mr. Cole, now shows us round. There is a yard surrounded by workshops, a smithy and sheds for storing timber. The planks of timber are laid with small gaps between them so that they will dry. That may take five years or more. Mr. Cole never gives his men unseasoned timber, and they would refuse to use it if he did.

In a corner of the yard is a brick-lined pit, about six feet deep. 'This is the saw pit,' explains Mr. Cole. 'One man goes into the pit and pulls the saw down, while one stands on the top and pulls it up. I was bottom sawyer as a young man. My face ran with sweat and was caked with sawdust, and all I had to look at was the brick wall. It's worse for the top sawyer though. His work is much harder, and he has to guide the saw.'

There is a smell of timber in the workshops and there are chippings and shavings on the floor. All

it. I then shape the ends of the spokes, and put on the felloes.' *'Is the wheel finished then?'* 'Not at all. We have to put on its tyre. If you like you can watch us do that in the morning.'

At six o'clock next morning we go to the wheelwright's shop. One man is lighting a furnace with a huge iron hoop in it. This is the tyre. It is six feet across and weighs about fifty pounds. Two men are fixing a wheel to the tyring platform. The platform is just a large iron plate on which the men clamp down the wheel. The boys trudge backwards and forwards from the pump, filling water buckets. There are several watering cans nearby.

The blacksmith has made the tyre about an inch and a half smaller than the wheel, so how will they fit it? The answer, of course, is that the tyre expands when it is red hot, and if everyone has done his work carefully, it should just slip over the rim of the wheel.

Soon everything is ready. There is a blast of hot air as Mr. Maggs opens the furnace. Three men grip the tyre with iron 'dogs', drop it into place and, working as fast as they can, drive it on with sledgehammers. The wood catches fire, so the boys spray it with water from the cans. The air is full of steam and smoke, and the men's eyes run. They still have to be very careful or they will spoil the wheel. When they finish, one of them trundles the wheel into a trough of water and there is a loud hissing. As the tyre cools it shrinks, forcing the spokes into their joints even more tightly than Mr. Maggs could with his sledge-

sorts of hand tools lie on the benches. The windows have no glass, just wooden shutters, which can be opened to let in the light. What must it be like in winter?

Mr. Cole tells us that the smith and the wheelwrights earn twenty-five shillings a week and the other men less than a pound. They work from six in the morning until seven in the evening. The men are proud of being craftsmen but they use the old ways which Mr. Cole thinks are too slow. He says he is losing money and will have to buy some machines or he will go out of business.

The Village Wheelwright

fixing the rim to a waggon wheel

4 The Wartime Farm

It is the year 1942. The Second World War has been raging for three years. German U-boats are sinking more and more shipping and Britain cannot import all the food she needs. It is essential that her farmers should produce all they can. We will visit a farm in Essex to see what is happening.

In the farmyard two girls are loading a trailer with manure. Suddenly a rat appears. They chase it into a corner and one of them kills it with a broom. Then she picks it up and throws it on the manure heap. *'Country girls aren't afraid of rats, then?'* 'We aren't country girls,' says one of them. 'We are typists, and we come from London.' *'What are you doing here?'* 'We are land girls for as long as the War lasts. We left our usual jobs to come down and work on this farm.' *'How do you like it?'* 'It's not bad once you get used to it. We were scared of mice in the beginning, but even the rats are scared of us now.'

The two girls hitch their trailer to a tractor and chug off to the fields. We go into the house to talk to Mr. Roe, the farmer. *'What are you doing to help the war effort, Mr. Roe?'* 'Trying to grow more food for the country, of course. This farm was in a shocking state when the War began. The ragwort grew so high you could get lost in it. Some of the hedges were thirty feet wide and twenty feet tall. Well, we have burnt the weeds, and we gained thirty acres, just by cutting back the hedges.' *'You are doing well, then?'*

Mr. Roe

'I could do a lot better if I were left alone, but the County War Agricultural Committee likes to tell us what to do. One of their men called to see me. He went over the farm and told me I would have to plough a lot of my land. But this soil is heavy clay, fit only for grass, as I explained to him. He replied that ploughed land feeds ten times as many people as grassland so I must plough it. When I told him my team of horses couldn't draw a plough through this clay, he promised to send me a tractor and some lime and some fertilizer to improve the poor soil. Then when I grumbled that I didn't have any labour because two of my men had joined the Army, he agreed to send me some labour. Well, the tractor, lime and fertilizer arrived, but do you know what the labour amounted to? Two London office girls, all dolled up with their silk stockings and nail varnish!'

'I still wasn't going to plough my fields, so they took me to court. I took a lump of clay and banged it on the table. "Who in their right mind would plough that?" I asked. The magistrate just said I must plough my land or he would have my farm taken away. I did plough it then. The clay turned up like putty, and then baked like bricks in the sun. It was a terrible job to break it down for sowing.' *'What happened?'* Mr Roe looks uncomfortable. 'Well,' he says, 'we did manage to grow a fair crop of oats.'

'How are the land girls managing?' 'Let's be fair,

they have come on very well. They do most of the farm jobs now. They grumble a bit, because they don't have much fun, but they don't know how to enjoy themselves in the country. They ought to come hunting with the rest of us.' *'Do you hunt in wartime?'* 'Why not? We've got to keep the foxes down somehow. People say hounds are too expensive to feed and we should spend the money on Spitfires. But what about the dogs townspeople keep? I say that the time to destroy the hounds is when all pet puppy dogs have been made into glue.'

'Are you making a good living on the farm, Mr. Roe?' 'Not too bad, thank you. It won't last, though, not once the War finishes. I can remember the First World War. "Grow all you can," they said, "and when the War is over we will make sure you always get a fair price for your goods." But almost as soon as the War ended they forgot their promise. The country was flooded with Canadian wheat, New Zealand lamb and Danish bacon. We just couldn't make a living. When I went into town I used to cross the road rather than go near my bank. I knew the manager was after me. One of my neighbours begged me to buy his land for £1 an acre, but I couldn't find the money. I would be a rich man now if I had. No, I just let this place become a wilderness as long as peace lasted. It will be the same again when this War ends, you mark my words.'

5 The Village Today

The village of Tarrant Upton is in West Dorset. The countryside around it is pleasant, but the village itself is unattractive. There is no manor house, no picturesque cottages, and the church is a very ordinary building, not much more than a hundred years old. Normally, tourists do not come here, and if any stray this far, they drive straight through.

We will walk along the village street in the middle of a summer day. Everything is still. There is no sign of life. Several of the houses must be empty, because their windows are boarded. The village pub is closed and there is a 'For Sale' sign outside. Further down the street is the church. It looks neglected, for the gravestones are nearly hidden in long grass. Here at last though, is someone to whom we can talk, for a little old lady is arranging flowers at the altar.

'Whatever is wrong with Tarrant Upton?' 'It's dying, that's what is wrong with it.' *'But why is it happening?'* 'Take this church for a start. When I was a girl there was a good congregation here for three services every Sunday – yes, and ringers to give us a peal of bells. Now the rector comes once a month and preaches to about four of us. The village school was closed because it was down to one teacher with a class of ten. Now there is a bus to take the children into Weymouth. Of course there are no tradesmen here, like plumbers, carpenters or painters. It's very difficult to get any jobs done. When my television broke down I had to telephone a man five miles away. He refused to come, because it wasn't worth his while.

'It was terrible when we lost our Post Office and general stores. Mrs. White who ran it said she just could not make a living. Now you can't even buy a postage stamp or a pound of sugar in Tarrant Upton. A few of the people have cars, so they shop in Weymouth, but I can't drive. Luckily one of my neighbours does my shopping for me.' *'Can't you go to Weymouth by bus?'* 'We used to have a bus three times a week. Then it came only on Saturdays. Now there isn't one at all.'

'What other problems do you find about living here?' 'The thing that really frightens me is that we have no doctor. Mine lives six miles away. If I was taken ill on a winter's night, I could be dead before he reached me. It's very difficult, too, when you need to get

medicines in a hurry.'

'What causes all these problems?' 'It's the farmers. They buy these huge machines, so they don't need so many men. A farmer can manage a big farm with his son and a couple of workers. The young men want jobs, so they move into town with their families. We old people are the only ones left. The farmers are ruining the countryside. When I was a girl, the banks were yellow with primroses, and you could sit in a field full of buttercups and celandines, with any number of pretty butterflies fluttering around. The farmers have killed all the flowers and insects with their horrid sprays. What's more, their great bulldozers are pulling up miles of hedges every year, and that destroys the wild life.'

We will now visit one of the farms. It is at the end of a long, private road, well made of concrete. The farmhouse is brand new. Behind it is a jumble of buildings and some new, expensive-looking machines. Mr. Hooper, the farmer, shows us round.

'You have spent a lot of money on machinery, Mr. Hooper.' 'Yes, indeed. That combine harvester alone cost me £14,000. It's worth it, though. You see, now I can manage this farm with three men. In the old days we needed a dozen.' 'But that means you are driving families from the village!' 'They insist on high wages, so I can only afford to pay a few.' 'An old lady in the village told us your sprays are killing all the wild flowers and insects.' 'I have to make a living from my farm, not keep it looking pretty for old ladies. Cows can't live on primroses and butterflies.' 'Why are you uprooting hedgerows?' 'They take up a lot of land and it makes a lot of work lopping them every year. Besides, I need big fields for my big machines.'

The saddest sight on Mr. Hooper's farm is the battery house. Here hundreds of hens are crowded three at a time in little cages. Mr. Hooper explains that this is the only way to make them lay enough eggs.

'Your farm seems very efficient, but it is certainly not very pleasant.' 'Now listen! British farmers could quite well scrap their machines, employ more men than they need, grow pretty hedgerows, and let their chickens run wild. And if they did, you towns-men would have to pay twice as much for your food as you do now.'

Work Section

Understand Your Work

1 The Farm Worker and his Family
1 Why is the Somerset and Dorset Railway useful for farmers?
2 Describe the surface of the country lane.
3 How many rooms are there in the Woodgets' cottage?
4 What cooking utensils does Mrs. Woodget have?
5 What food does she cook?
6 What is Mrs. Woodget's full-time job, most of the year?
7 What is the family income?
8 What does Mrs. Woodget buy with it?
9 What food can the family provide for itself?
10 In what other ways does the family make up for its low income?
11 Why is Mr. Woodget healthy?
12 What is likely to happen to him one day?
13 Which is the busiest time of the year for him?
14 What especially skilled work does Mr. Woodget do?
15 What happens when the weather is bad?
16 What does George Woodget wear?
17 Make a list of some of the jobs George does on the farm.
18 What does George eat for breakfast and dinner?
19 Why is George frightened to walk home?
20 Why does George have little time to enjoy himself?

2 The Farmer
1 How do the Goughs use their kitchen?
2 How had it been used a hundred years earlier?
3 Why is Mrs. Gough's maid unhappy?
4 What is her ambition?
5 How do the farmers spend their evenings?
6 How do they travel?
7 What happens at the local fairs?
8 Why do the fairs worry Mr. Gough?
9 What do Mr. and Mrs. Gough wear to church?
10 Whereabouts do the villagers sit in church?
11 How many cows does Mr. Gough have?
12 What modern equipment does he have on his farm?
13 What is Mrs. Gough's work on the farm?
14 Why doesn't Mr. Gough produce wheat or meat?
15 What does he do with most of his milk?
16 What crops does he grow?
17 What happens to all his crops?
18 Why will he not buy machines?
19 What excuse does he make for paying low wages?
20 What animals does he breed, as a sideline?

3 The Village Wheelwright
1 What things does a wheelwright make?
2 What is the piece at the centre of a wheel called? How is it shaped?

3 How are the spokes shaped?
4 What are felloes?
5 How much smaller is the tyre than the wheel?
6 Why is it possible to fit it?
7 What does the tyre do to the wheel as it cools and shrinks?
8 How are trees sawn into planks?
9 Why is Mr. Cole losing money?
10 How can he stop this happening?

4 The Wartime Farm
1 Why did Britain need to produce a lot of food during the War?
2 What were 'land girls'?
3 How has Mr. Roe improved his farm since War began?
4 What instructions did the County War Agricultural Committee give him?
5 What help did they offer?
6 Why did Mr. Roe object?
7 Was he right to do so?
8 What had the Government promised farmers during the First World War?
9 Why were farmers poor between the Wars?
10 What does Mr. Roe think will happen when the Second World War is over?

5 The Village Today
1 How can you tell that families are leaving Tarrant Upton?
2 What problems are there for those who remain?
3 Why are the farmers to blame?
4 How, according to the old lady, are farmers ruining the countryside?
5 How can you tell Mr. Hooper is rich?
6 Why does he buy expensive machines?
7 Why does he spray his crops?
8 Why is he uprooting hedges?
9 Where does Mr. Hooper keep his hens? Why?
10 How does Mr. Hooper's way of farming benefit the rest of us?

Use Your Imagination

1 You are a farm worker's daughter who has become a domestic servant. Explain why you were glad to leave home. (1)
2 Write a story about a farm boy who lived in Victorian times. (1)
3 A farm labourer goes to his employer to ask for higher wages and they start an argument. Write what they say. (1, 2)
4 Imagine you are staying with Mr. and Mrs. Gough, as a visitor. Write a letter to your parents describing life on the farm. (2)
5 Draw up a list of instructions for making a wheel. (3)
6 You are a land girl on Mr. Roe's farm. Say what happened and how you felt, the first day you arrived. (4)
7 You are an inspector from the County War Agricultural Committee. Write a report on Mr. Roe's farm, saying what changes have been made there since the War began. (4)
8 You are living at Tarrant Upton. Write a letter to the County Council to persuade them to help your village. (5)
9 In the eighteenth century Oliver Goldsmith wrote a poem called 'The Deserted Village'. Write one of your own with the same title about a modern village. (5)
10 Make a list of the changes that have taken place in the countryside over the last hundred years. List the advantages and disadvantages. (All sections)

Further Work

1 Look for the following in museums, or find pictures of them in books:
   (a) farm equipment and machinery;
   (b) cottage furniture and cooking utensils;
   (c) wheelwrights' tools.
2 Read some chapters in *Lark Rise to Candleford* by Flora Thompson.
3 Find out about village craftsmen in Victorian times, other than wheelwrights, e.g. the blacksmith and the thatcher.
4 How did farming develop on the North American Prairies and in New Zealand? How did the changes there affect British farmers?
5 Apart from Cheddar, what other English cheeses are there? How are they made?
6 What changes have there been in the English village over the last hundred years in a) housing; b) transport; c) education; d) amusements? Any pictures you can find of village life will help you.
7 Make a list of the machines you might find on a farm today. Describe the use of each one.
8 Find out what was done to grow more food in Britain during both World Wars.
9 What different breeds of cattle do farmers keep today? What are the advantages of each?
10 In your trips round the countryside, make a note of the crops you see growing. Find out the names of any you do not recognize, and why they are grown.

Chapter Five   People and Their Rights

1 Care of the Poor

Mr. Walker is one of the Guardians of the Poor in Bath. He will tell us what he does. *'How did you become a Guardian, Mr. Walker?'* 'I was elected with about twenty other men. The ratepayers voted for us. We have a meeting once a month.' *'Is it a bit like being elected to the City Council?'* 'Yes, except that the City Council deals with all sorts of things. Guardians just look after the poor, nothing else.' *'What have you done for the poor in Bath?'* 'We have built a fine workhouse on Combe Down. We pay a workhouse master to run it, we pay a local doctor to visit it regularly, and we even pay a schoolmaster to teach the children.'

'Why is it that so many poor people in Bath would sooner starve than go to the workhouse?' 'We do nothing to make the workhouse comfortable. The paupers have to wear a uniform, we give them only the plainest food, mainly bread and gruel, and the men and women have to live separately. No one has any beer or tobacco and we will not let relatives send in things like cakes or puddings. We find the inmates plenty of dull work. The men crack stones and the women wash clothes. Life must be made more unpleasant in the workhouse than outside, or people would flock there in their hundreds. The workhouse costs the ratepayers enough as it is.'

'Is that all you do for the poor in Bath?' 'Oh no, there are plenty of charities as well. I give money to a soup charity myself. When food is scarce, as it was last winter, we open a soup kitchen in Walcot. Those of us who have paid money towards the kitchen give out tickets to poor people of our choice. They can go to the kitchen and exchange the tickets for soup. We only give tickets to the deserving poor, of course. We do not aim to feed drunkards and idlers. There are other charities for milk, bread and coal. You can be sure that the wealthier citizens of Bath look after their poor.' *'But we have found families in the Dolemeads living in slums, and starving.'* 'That is their own fault. They drink too much and throw their money away on stupid things. They never

Dr. Barnado

think of saving. Most of them are wicked and their unhappiness is God's way of punishing them. Besides, it is quite a good thing for some of the lower classes to live in misery. The others see them, and it makes them work harder. It is quite certain that there will always be some poor people. It says in the Bible, "The poor ye have always with ye." '

Luckily, not everyone was like Mr. Walker. In 1866 a young Irish medical student came to London. He opened a school for poor boys in an old donkey stable at Hope's Place, World's End, in the East End of London. During the evenings he taught there while the other students enjoyed themselves. One day, a wretched, starving boy called Jim Jarvis refused to leave when the lessons were over. He had nowhere to go. The teacher took him home and while Jim was enjoying the first good meal he had ever eaten, he told his life story. He could not remember his father but could just remember his mother as she lay dying. Jim had been taken to the workhouse but hated it so much that he ran away. For a time he lived in a garden shed belonging to an old woman. Then, when he was about seven, he worked for a bargee called Swearing Dick. Dick was a drunkard who beat Jim cruelly. He had a fierce dog and threatened to send him after Jim if he ever tried to escape. Jim did escape in the end, and for the next three years he lived in the streets of London. By begging and doing odd jobs he managed to stay alive, but nearly every night, winter and summer, he had to sleep in the open.

At first the medical student refused to believe that there were children who had no homes, but Jim took him out into the night. They came to a dark street and climbed a high wall. At the top was a tin roof, and on it were eleven boys, just like Jim, all fast asleep. The student was horrified. He found somewhere for Jim to live and decided that he must spend the rest of his life doing the same for other homeless children. He needed money, of course, and the first person to give him any was a servant girl who let him have all her savings, twenty-seven farthings (about three pence). By the time he died in 1905, he had raised three million pounds and helped 168,000 boys and girls. His name was Doctor Barnardo.

There came a time, too, when the Government saw that it could not leave the care of the poor to Guardians like Mr. Walker. It was arranged that money should be paid to people when they were ill or unemployed, and in 1908 pensions were given to old people. A pensioner had to be seventy years of age

a homeless girl

same girl after rescue by Dr Barnardo

and received only five shillings a week. Even so, many old people could not believe their good luck. All they knew was that they were very grateful. Some of them took flowers for the postmistress when they went to collect their pensions.

Votes for Women

Emily Davidson throwing herself in front of the King's horse in the 1913 Derby

5 Immigrants

Many of the people of Bedford are immigrants. They have come from the West Indies, India, Pakistan and various parts of Europe. In 1970, there were 7,000 Italians in the town. This was ten per cent of the population. A manager of the local brickworks will tell us about them.

'Bedford stands on a thick layer of clay. It is perfect for making bricks, but the work is very hard and unpleasant. We have always found it difficult to persuade people to do it. Well, back in 1950 we heard there was a lot of unemployment in Southern Italy, so some of us went to Naples to see if there were any Italians who would like to work in the brickfields. When they heard what good wages we were paying, they were very keen to come. We were glad to have them. They were used to a rough life and they didn't complain about the work. The only trouble was that the best ones left after a while. Some have started their own businesses. A few sell ice-cream, and others are hairdressers or grocers.' *'How did the Italians get on with the people of Bedford?'* 'Very well, on the whole. Italians are clean and hard-working, and they keep out of trouble. What more do you want?' *'Don't you think you ran a big risk, bringing so many foreigners to an English town?'* 'English people would soon complain if there were no bricks to build houses. If they won't make the bricks themselves, foreigners must

Italian brickmakers in Bedford

do it for them.'

We will now talk to a Roman Catholic priest who is himself an Italian. *'What work do you do for the immigrants, Father?'* 'I have to help in all kinds of ways. I don't think the English understand half the forms they have to fill in, so you can imagine how difficult strangers find them. I do my best to see they have jobs, and houses, and I act as interpreter when necessary. They must not forget they are Italians, so we have a youth club for the young people and another club for the grown-ups. That one has a bocca court, so they can play a real Italian game. My main task is to see that they are good Catholics, and bring up their children in the Faith. We have built a beautiful church dedicated to Saint Francesca Cabrini. She spent her life working for emigrants. There is plenty to do. Twenty-five million Italians left their country in the last hundred years.' *'Why was that?'* 'Most of them came from Southern Italy and Sicily, and they were desperately poor. They lived in little hovels, in villages almost cut off from the rest of the world. The soil is thin and poor, there is hardly any rain, and it is as hot as North Africa in the summer. The men who came here only wanted to make

a village in Sicily

money. They didn't mind working in the brickfields as long as they could scrape together enough money to bring over their families. At first they crowded together in lodgings, but most of them have their own houses now.'

'*How do the Italians get on with the people of Bedford?*' 'There were problems at first. You see, Italians can hardly ever talk quietly. They shout and wave their arms around. They don't stay inside on summer evenings, but flock into the streets. They love to have their radios playing loudly, so the air is full of noise, to say nothing of the smell of cooking. That's how people behave in Italy, but English neighbours found it hard to accept. Fortunately there have been no serious problems, such as violence.' '*Is that because the Italians have learnt English ways?*' 'Not at all. They keep out of trouble, by keeping themselves to themselves. They have their own part of the town. Mostly they only talk to each other. Not many speak English at all well – just enough to get by.'

We will now meet an Italian boy called Marco. He is fifteen and was born in Bedford. '*Do you want to go back to Italy, Marco?*' 'My parents have taken me back on holiday, but I could never live there. The village in Italy was so boring because there was nothing at all to do. I am hoping to get an engineering apprenticeship when I leave school but there are no jobs of that kind in my parents' village.' '*Do you enjoy life in England?*' 'I can't say it's easy. I am at school with English boys, and I like to go around with the gang. They go to football matches, they smoke and drink, and one or two are trying drugs. If I don't do the same, they call me "chicken". They don't understand how easy it is to upset Italian parents. My father thinks his word is law. If I want to go out he asks where I am going, what I am going to do and who I am going with. He always wants to know when I will be back. Sometimes he just sits in front of the television and tells me I must stay in. My English friends don't have to put up with that. They come and go as they like and they laugh at me because I am scared of my father. But it's even worse for my sister. She is eighteen and works in an office, but my parents only let her go out one evening a week. On the other evenings she must stay in and spend her time helping with the housework. My parents even say that when she marries it must be to a boy they choose. They are scared she will do like one of my cousins who went off to live with a man who isn't even a Catholic. My mother says she has disgraced the whole family – grandparents, uncles, aunts, cousins, everyone.' '*How do you feel about her, Marco?*' ' "Good luck to her", is what I say!'

four generations of the Spadaccino family, originally from Italy, now settled in Bedford

Work Section

Understand Your Work

1 Care of the Poor

1 How did Mr. Walker become a Poor Law Guardian?
2 What did the Poor Law Guardians do for the poor?
3 Who provided the money?
4 Why did the poor people dislike the workhouse?
5 What did the charities in Bath give to the poor?
6 According to Mr. Walker, why did people become poor?
7 What did Dr. Barnardo do in his spare time, when he first came to London?
8 What did Jim Jarvis show him one night?
9 What did Dr. Barnardo decide to do as a result?
10 What did the Government do for old people in 1908?

2 The Welfare State

1 What did the Government ask Sir William Beveridge to do in 1941?
2 According to Beveridge, what was Britain's most serious problem?
3 Who pays into the National Insurance Fund?
4 What happens when people are ill, or out of work?
5 What other help is given by the Welfare State?
6 List five other problems that Beveridge mentioned and say how he thought each one could be solved.
7 When did Parliament pass laws to create the Welfare State?
8 What is the basic idea behind the Welfare State?
9 Make a list of the ways in which Mrs. Groves and her family were helped by the Welfare State.
10 What was she expecting to have from the local council?

3 Votes for Women

1 Why were women not allowed to vote?
2 What was a 'suffragette'?
3 What was the slogan of the suffragettes?
4 Name some of the things they did in order to win the vote.
5 What happened to Emily Davison?
6 What was the 'Cat and Mouse Act'?
7 What work did women do during the War?
8 What did this prove?
9 What did Parliament do about giving women the vote in 1918 and in 1928?
10 In what other ways have women won equality with men?

4 The General Strike 1926

1 Why did the miners think they should have good wages?
2 What did the coal owners ask them to do?
3 How did the miners think the Government should help?
4 What did the men in other trade unions do to help the miners?
5 What did the Prime Minister ask people to do before the strike?
6 Why did Mr. Brown object to the general strike?
7 What things were done to defeat the strike?

8 Why did the Trades Union Congress call an end to the general strike?
9 How long had the strike lasted?
10 How long did the miners stay on strike? What did they have to do when the strike was over?

5 Immigrants

1 When immigrants move into an English town what rights are claimed by: a) the immigrants; b) the English; c) the children of the immigrants?
2 Why did many Italians move to Bedford in the 1950s? What work do they do there?
3 What help does the Roman Catholic priest give the Italians in Bedford?
4 What does he see as his most important duty?
5 How many Italians emigrated over the last hundred years?
6 From which part of Italy did most of them leave?
7 Which of the Italians' habits annoyed the people of Bedford?
8 Why have the Italians not learnt English ways?
9 What rules do Italian fathers make for their children?
10 What problems do these rules create for the Italian children?

Use Your Imagination

1 You are a poor person living in Bath in 1890. Say why you think you are badly treated. (1)
2 Write a story about a boy who was rescued by Dr. Barnardo. (1)
3 You are Sir William Beveridge. Write a report for the Government suggesting it should make Britain a Welfare State and saying how it could be done. (2)
4 Two people have an argument. One is in favour of the welfare state, the other thinks it does too much for people. Write what they say (2)
5 You are a Member of Parliament in 1912. Say why you do not believe in giving women the vote, and what you think of suffragettes. (3)
6 You are the same Member of Parliament in 1918. Explain why you have voted for the law which gives women the vote. (3)
7 You are Mr. Baldwin. It is early in 1926 and you can see that a general strike is likely. Make a list of the things you want done so that the country will be prepared for the strike. (4)
8 Mr. Evans and Mr. Brown meet after the general strike and have an argument. Write what they say. (4)
9 An Italian father forbids his son to go out in the evening and they start an argument. Write what they say. (5)
10 Write a story about an Italian boy or girl who comes to live in Bedford. (5)

Further Work

1 Read more about nineteenth century workhouses.
2 Find out more about Dr. Barnardo, and the lives of some of the children he helped.
3 Ask your parents how much they pay in National Insurance contributions and what they think about the Welfare State.
4 List the ways in which you and members of your family have had help from the Welfare State.
5 Find out: a) Who was the first woman Member of Parliament.
b) When she was elected.
c) Which members of the Cabinet of the present Government are women, and what posts they hold.
6 Apart from gaining the right to vote, a woman's lot has improved a great deal over the last hundred years. In what ways has this happened?
7 Read more about the history of the trade unions, both before and since the general strike.
8 Speak to any grown-up you know who is a member of a trade union. Ask him how he expects his union to help him.
9 List the countries from which immigrants have come to Britain since the 1950s. Find out why they left their homes.
10 Find out what is being done today to solve the problems caused by immigration.

Chapter 6 Britain at War

1 Dreadnought

It is the year 1906. We will visit Admiral Sir John Fisher. He is the First Sea Lord, which means he is the most important man in the Royal Navy. He tells us what he has done for the Navy.

'Let's just go back to 1897. That was the year of Queen Victoria's Diamond Jubilee. There was a splendid naval review at Spithead, you remember, and I must say the fleet certainly *looked* fine. All the paintwork was clean and new, and the brasswork was shining. There were 165 ships in three lines each 30 miles long, and that was just the home fleet. We had as many ships again guarding the Empire all over the world. We made sure our fleet was as big as the two largest foreign navies put together. The "two-power standard" we called it. No wonder foreigners were jealous. "Rule Britannia," we sang, "Britannia rule the waves!" Some of us knew better though. Admiral Beresford put his finger on it, "The fleet is not ready to fight, or nearly ready to fight," is what he said. I agreed with him.

'The Russians had a fleet like ours — a lot smaller of course, but the same kind of vessel. You know what happened when they fought against the splendid modern ships of the Japanese navy. The Japanese sank nearly the whole fleet in just one battle. The same thing would have happened to *us* if we had been foolish enough to fight.'

'What was wrong with the British fleet, Sir John?' 'Well, in the first place, there were too many useless old ships. Do you know that there were some old tubs at the Spithead review that had to be towed there? Did you hear about H.M.S. *Galatea?* That was a ship we had on service in the Far East. There was nothing wrong with the shine on her brass, but she was full of rot and rust. She was also full of dead rats and cockroaches. When at last they got round to clearing out her holds it took a gang several days to shovel out all the corpses.

'We didn't take care of the sailors either. Their lavatories stank and the air in their quarters was so stuffy they could hardly breathe. In winter they froze, and in summer they were nearly cooked alive. Do you know, we didn't even give them knives and forks! They used to eat with clasp knives and their fingers.'

'What frightens me most,' continues Sir John, 'is

Spithead review, 1897

to remember how bad the naval gunnery was. They could only put one shot in three on the target. The crews used to practise cutlass drill. I have no doubt that they would have done very well in cutlass fights, but in modern navies we fight with guns and torpedoes. That's another thing. The admirals didn't seem to know about the torpedo, even though it was an English invention. Foreigners knew about it and they knew about submarines, too. As for our people, Admiral Wilson was typical. He used to say that submarines weren't proper weapons of war, and that if he caught any he would hang their crews as pirates.

'Well, I've put a stop to all that nonsense. I've scrapped any number of old ships, and saved money for better uses. I've got rid of a lot of useless people too. The sailors are a lot more comfortable now. They have knives and forks. There are bakeries on the ships as well, so they have bread to eat instead of "hard-tack" – you know, those things that looked like oversized dog biscuits, but tasted worse. Have you heard of the Royal Naval College at Dartmouth? I started that. What's more, we let ordinary lads go there, as long as they are clever enough. It's no use making a man an officer, just because his father is a gentleman. Because you have breeding, it doesn't

cutlass drill

mean you must have brains. Ships have practised their gunnery too, until they are sick of it. They hit the target much more often these days.

'All that is nothing compared with my new ship. My motto is "Hit first! Hit hard! Keep on hitting!", but we didn't have the ships that could do that. We do now. People wanted me to go carefully and try all sorts of experiments with models, but I say that the best scale for experiments is twelve inches to the foot. I made them get on with it, and the builders finished my new ship in just a year and a day. Now every other battleship in the world is out of date.'

the *Dreadnought*

'What do you call this wonderful new ship, Sir John?' 'Well, I don't expect you've counted, but the words "Fear not" appear in the Bible eighty times. That gave me the idea. We call the ship *Dreadnought*. What makes her so good? There are her guns for one thing. Other battleships have four twelve-inch guns. *Dreadnought* has ten. Even if an enemy managed to hit her, it wouldn't do much damage. On the waterline, where it matters, she has armour plate eleven inches thick. She is heavy, of course, some 18,000 tons, but she is fast. She is the first battleship to have Parsons turbines instead of piston engines and can do 22 knots.'

'What would happen if the *Dreadnought* took part in a battle?' 'In a battle the *Dreadnought* would train all her guns on the waterline of the enemy ship and blast a hole in it with eight tons of shells. Then she would deal with the next ship and the next, and the next. She can out-sail and out-gun anything afloat,' replies Sir John.

2 Jutland

You saw in the last section how Admiral Fisher built the *Dreadnought* and how it made every other battleship in the world out of date. But there was a problem. Not only were all foreign battleships out of date, but so were all other British ships as well. The Germans realized this. They began to build Dreadnoughts of their own, and all the old British battleships became useless. The only thing the British could do was to build more Dreadnoughts than the Germans. Luckily, Britain was able to win this ship-building race, because the Germans had to concentrate more on their army. None the less, the German navy was a powerful modern force, and the British were scared of it.

The First World War began in 1914. At that time, most of the German High Seas Fleet was in its harbours in North Germany, while the British Grand Fleet was at Scapa Flow in the Orkneys. They were there to stop the Germans from sailing round the north of Scotland and into the Atlantic. If they had done that, they would have been able to sink the merchant ships bringing Britain the food and supplies she needed to fight the war. The British admiral, Sir John Jellicoe, was worried. He knew that the Germans had dangerous new weapons – mines, torpedoes and submarines. He knew also that if the Germans destroyed his ships they could at once invade Britain with a large army and they could easily win the War. Sir Winston Churchill said that Jellicoe 'was the only man who could lose the War in an afternoon.' No

John Cornwall by his gun

wonder Admiral Jellicoe was careful! On the other hand, the Germans saw that the British outnumbered them by two to one, so they were not anxious to have a battle. Both sides wondered what to do. For a long time they did nothing.

What the Germans wanted was to catch a part of the British fleet on its own. In May 1916 they thought their chance had come. Admiral Scheer led their High Seas Fleet after a squadron of battle cruisers commanded by Admiral Beatty. Scheer then discovered to his horror that the whole of the British Grand Fleet was close by. What was worse, Jellicoe's ships were between him and his home ports. The Germans had to fight. The battle that followed is known as the Battle of Jutland.

Every man in the British fleet had been longing for the day when they would at last meet the German fleet and destroy it. They thought it would be a second Trafalgar, a great victory for the British. However, Jutland was not at all like that. There was plenty of action. When a Dreadnought fired all her guns, her stokehold filled with coal dust, and the crockery flew everywhere. As shells came crashing into the ships

map of the Battle of Jutland

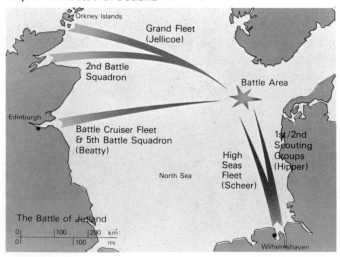

on both sides, more and more men were killed or wounded. On one of the British ships John Cornwell, a boy of sixteen, was mortally wounded. He stayed by his post while the rest of the gun crew lay dead and dying around him. He was given a posthumous V.C.

Few of the sailors could see what was happening, so on another British ship a young officer they called Mr. Johnston gave his men a running commentary and handed round mugs of tea. Mr. Johnston was really Prince George, the future George VI and the father of our Queen Elizabeth.

The battle did not go well for the British. Three of their battle cruisers blew up, which happened all too easily because they were badly designed. On the other hand, the German ships were difficult to sink because they were so well built. The British gunners were not nearly as accurate as the enemy gunners. The Germans scored far more hits. Many of the British shells were duds and did not explode as they should have done. The great battleships were frightened of the little German destroyers. They had good reason, because the destroyers fired torpedoes which could do more damage than the biggest guns.

At the start of the battle, the British had the Germans in a trap, and they outnumbered them two to one. However, the Germans fought so well that they were able to escape. Not only that, they lost far less shipping than the British and less than half as many men. None the less both fleets were almost as strong after the battle as they had been before, because, of the 250 ships that took part, only 25 were sunk. The Germans went back to their ports, and the British went back to Scapa Flow. Neither navy did

very much surface fighting after Jutland.

However the German navy did come near to winning the War, and Jellicoe came near to losing it, though not in an afternoon. While the German High Seas Fleet stayed safely at home, German U-boats, or submarines, went all over the Atlantic. They sank so many merchant ships that it looked as if Britain would run out of food supplies and starve. The only sensible thing was to put the merchant ships in convoys and protect them with warships. At first Jellicoe refused to do this. He said that if large numbers of merchant ships sailed together then the U-boats would be able to sink even more of them. What he did not realize was that if the U-boats attacked a convoy they would have to sail close to the warships defending it. That meant the warships could find the U-boats and destroy them, which they had not been able to do before. In April 1917, the British lost 420 merchant ships. At last Jellicoe allowed convoys and from that time far fewer merchant ships were sunk.

You might like to know what happened to Admiral Fisher's *Dreadnought*. She was in harbour for repairs at the time of the Battle of Jutland. She did very little all through the War, and was scrapped in 1922.

What happened to the German High Seas Fleet? When the War ended the Germans were ordered to send it to Scapa Flow to surrender. The sailors took the ships to Scapa Flow but were determined that the British should not have their splendid fleet. When they arrived they opened the sea cocks and their ships filled with water. Every one of them sank to the bottom.

5 The Battle of Britain

After the First World War ended, there were twenty years of peace. In 1933, the Germans found a new leader – Adolph Hitler. He promised he would make Germany a great country once more, and take revenge for the Treaty of Versailles. First he seized Austria, then Czechoslovakia, but when he attacked Poland, the French and the British decided they must stop him. They told him he must leave Poland alone or they would fight. Hitler ignored them, and the Second World War began.

War broke out in September 1939. By the summer of 1940 the Germans had not only defeated Poland, but France as well. They were now wondering how to conquer Britain. The Germans knew they could defeat the British Army easily if they could only cross the English Channel. But they only had barges to carry their men across and the Channel was alive with ships of the Royal Navy. A man who thought he had the answer to this problem was Hermann Goering. Goering had been a fighter pilot in the First World War, and now he was in command of the German air force. Only a few weeks before, Goering's aeroplanes had destroyed the town of Rotterdam, frightening the Dutch into surrender. He was sure that Britain, too, could be defeated from the air. His bombers could do this, but he could not send them on their own because they flew too slowly to escape the British fighter planes. That did not matter, though, because Goering could protect his bombers with his own fighters. He had hundreds of *Messerschmitt 109s, and he thought they were the best fighter planes in the world.

From July 1940 onwards, German aircraft attacked Britain again and again. They soon realized that they were not going to win easily. For one thing, the British always seemed to know they were coming and were ready for them. This was because the British had radar. They had built huge aerials which sent out signals. If the signals met nothing, they just vanished into the atmosphere. But if they hit an aircraft they rebounded like a ball flung against a wall. A signal then showed up in the radar station on an instrument rather like a television screen, and so gave warning that the Germans were on their way. The British had excellent fighter planes, Hurricanes and Spitfires. We will talk to Kenneth, a fighter pilot who flies a Spitfire.

'*How does your Spitfire compare with a Messerschmitt?*' 'Not badly; the German planes have two cannons and two machine guns, and Spitfires have eight machine guns, so they are about equal. Both aircraft can fly at about 400 m.p.h. I'm afraid that the Messerschmitt is better really high up. Height is very important for a fighter pilot: he likes to be able to dive down on his enemy. Above 30,000 feet, the Spitfire can't climb at all quickly, and the engine often misses a beat. I was left behind by my squadron the other day. It was frightening. The Germans like to "bounce" a stray aircraft. It was bitterly cold, and my cockpit cover steamed over, so I could hardly see a thing. Anyway, if the Germans attack, they usually fly out of the sun. I'd have been dazzled and wouldn't have spotted them until it was too late.'

'*How good are the German pilots?*' 'Much better than the British on the whole. They have all been flying and fighting for a long time. Too many of the British pilots are like me, not properly trained at all. It is as much as I can do to fly my Spitfire, let alone shoot down Germans.' '*What are you most afraid of?*'

a Hurricane fighter

*Willy Messerschmitt, the designer of this brilliant fighter plane, 112 lived to be a very old man and did not die until September 1978.

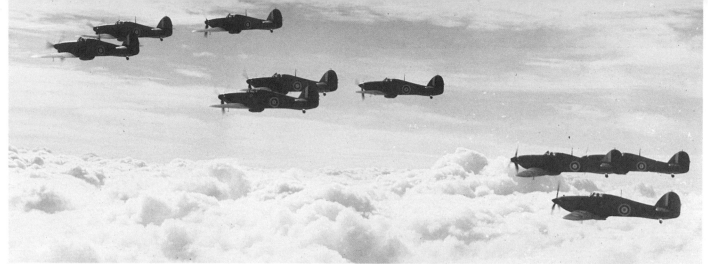
Hurricanes in flight

'Being burnt to death. The petrol tank is just in front of the cockpit. I always carry a pistol, and if ever the petrol catches fire, I shall shoot myself.' *Do you think we are going to win?* 'I doubt it. The trouble is I don't think Air Marshall Dowding knows what he is doing. He sends just a few of us into battle at a time. We are heavily outnumbered, but there are plenty of aircraft left on the ground doing nothing. Lots of our best pilots have been killed and we are all tired. I have seen a man fall asleep over his breakfast. He was snoring away with his face in his fried egg. Just now the Germans are attacking our airfields and when they put those out of action we are finished.'

Luckily, Ken was wrong. The Germans did not win the Battle of Britain. Why was that?

For one thing, Air Chief Marshal Sir Hugh Dowding, the man in charge of the R.A.F., knew very much what he was doing. He realized that as soon as autumn came, the weather would be too bad for the Germans to invade. In the meantime, what he had to do was to stop the Germans from destroying his

operations room of RAF Fighter Command

a German fighter shot down over southern England

fighter planes. That was why he sent them into battle only a few at a time.

Another important man was Lord Beaverbrook. His job was to see the factories made enough fighter planes. Soon we were making 400 a month in Britain, while the Germans were only making 140. Unfortunately no one could produce fighter pilots nearly as quickly.

The two men who really saved Britain in 1940 were Hitler and Goering! The reason was that they made a serious mistake. Ken was quite right when he said the Germans would win if they went on attacking airfields. However, the British bombed Berlin and Hitler and Goering wanted revenge. They ordered their airmen to leave the airfields alone and bomb London instead. The Germans attacked day and night and soon large parts of the city were blazing. Their biggest attack was on September 15th when 1,000 aeroplanes set out for London. The R.A.F. drove them back after some fierce fighting. We now call September 15th Battle of Britain Day. Really, the Battle of Britain was won as soon as the Germans decided to attack the ordinary people of London, rather than destroy the fighter planes of the R.A.F.

The Battle of Britain

a painting by Paul Nash depicting the Battle of Britain

6 The War in the Desert

From 1940 to 1943 the British Eighth Army was fighting the Germans and the Italians in the Western Desert of North Africa. The desert is a dreadful place. There is sand in places, and rocks as well, but most of it is just dust. From time to time the wind blows the dust into great billowing clouds. Vehicles on the move make their own little sandstorms as well. Here and there are mounds, but they are so low you can hardly call them hills. The most striking things are the depressions, huge pits in the ground, with sides like cliffs. The largest of these, the Qattara Depression, is 400 feet deep and 200 miles long. Maps of many parts of the desert are just blank sheets of paper. There is nothing to plot. Hundreds of square miles are empty and desolate. The climate is unpleasant. Early morning may not be too bad, but by midday the heat is unbearable. Towards sunset there is often a sandstorm. The nights are cold.

Why should anyone want to defend the Western Desert? The answer is that beyond the desert lay Egypt, the Suez Canal and the Middle East. Germany was short of oil, but if she conquered the Middle East and all its oilfields she could have all the oil she needed.

At first, the British had only the Italians to fight. The Italians were not cowards, but they had bad generals and bad equipment. In two months the British captured 130,000 Italians and lost less than 2,000 men themselves. Then General Rommel arrived with the German Afrika Korps. He drove the British back 500 miles, almost to the River Nile.

We will now talk to Bob, a commander of a tank, who is on leave in Cairo.

'*What is it like fighting in the desert?*' 'My father fought in the trenches in the First World War. He seems to have spent most of his time up to his knees in mud. At least we are spared that. We have dust rather than mud. It gets into our food, our clothes, our hair and our tank. Most of the time I have my head out of the top of the tank, so by the end of the day I am covered with dust. The heat is bad, too. You can fry an egg on the tank at noon. I know because I have done it. The flies are the worst thing. They get all over the food, they crawl up your nose, into your

a Crusader Mark II tank in the desert

an American Sherman Mark II tank

shot weighing only two pounds and the range is only about 600 yards. To make things even worse, Rommel has some nasty new weapons. The Germans are planting mines all over the place. "Devil's Eggs", they call them. The only way to find them is to send infantry to prod the ground with bayonets. How would you like to do that with the enemy shelling you? Rommel also has some deadly anti-tank guns. I have known one of them pick off half a dozen of our tanks on its own. What bothers me most is that no one seems to be in charge any more. The Eighth Army is breaking up, and each bit is fighting its own little war and losing it.' *'Are we going to be beaten then, Bob?'* 'If things go on like this, yes. But give us some good tanks and a good general and we will chase the Germans out of Africa.'

mouth and round the corner of your eyes. They are after the moisture you see. They will drink the sweat off your back. I have seen marching soldiers black with them. What the flies like best is blood. They swarm round the slightest cut and heaven help you if you are left wounded in the desert!'

'What do you eat?' 'Bully beef and biscuits most of the time. We have tinned milk and tea. To brew up we make a "desert fire" from sand soaked in petrol. Things were better when we were chasing the Italians. We used to capture their tinned tomatoes and vegetables. They had plenty of wine, too. Our big problem is water. Sometimes we are down to half a gallon a day each. That has to do for drinking, washing and the radiator of the tank.'

'I expect you feel safe in your tank, don't you?' 'Safe? If you had seen a roasted body hanging out of a tank, you would know how safe we feel. We are safe against a man with a rifle and that is about all. My Crusader has some thick armour at the front, but not at the sides. It is easy enough to blow off a track, and then we are stranded. What we dread most is being hit in the petrol tank, or even worse, the ammunition locker. If that happens the tank is a blazing inferno within seconds and there is no hope of getting out alive.'

'Why have the Germans defeated you so easily?' 'They have much better weapons. Take my Crusader. It *looks* strong enough, but it is always breaking down. The gun is almost useless. It throws a solid

Montgomery

In fact, both the things Bob wanted were on their way. The Americans sent 300 Sherman tanks that were more than a match for the ones the Germans had. General Bernard Montgomery took charge of the Eighth Army. On October 23rd, 1942 the Battle of El Alamein began. After more than two weeks of fierce fighting the Germans were defeated. In May the following year Rommel withdrew to Italy with the remains of his army.

117

7 Convoy

In Autumn 1942, some thirty ships were steaming down the St. Lawrence River. Others were coming from New York, Halifax and Cape Breton Island. Together there were over a hundred of them, all heading for a stretch of empty water near Newfoundland. They were going to form a convoy, one of the many that brought the food, weapons and other supplies that Britain needed to fight the war against Germany.

The great damage to shipping came from submarines, or U-boats. Germany had conquered France in 1940 and was able to use French ports. The U-boats could sail anywhere they wished in the Atlantic. Usually, they hunted in groups called 'wolf-packs'. In the second section you saw that during the First World War thousands of lives and hundreds of ships were lost in the Atlantic, and for a long time Admiral Jellicoe refused to allow convoys. The British had learnt their lesson over those terrible losses, and started convoys as soon as the Second World War began. Even so, the U-boats still managed to sink nearly 300 ships during the six years of war.

We will now see what happened to our convoy off Newfoundland. Each ship had a number, and as

a U-boat in the Atlantic

it arrived it took its proper place. You can see how they were arranged in the diagram:

11	21	31	41	51
12	22	32	42	52
13	23	33	43	53
14	24	34	44	54
15	25	35	45	55

You will see that ship 14 was in row 4 of column 1, and ship 31, which was the 'Commodore' ship was in row 1 of column 3, the middle column. The Commodore was an officer of the Royal Navy who had charge of the merchant ships, though he had to take orders from the Senior Naval Officer who was in charge of the escort. There were eighteen warships to protect the convoy, little ships, such as corvettes and frigates which were deadly to the U-boats. Six of the escort ships stayed close to the convoy, while the rest stayed far out, hoping to catch the U-boats before they could get close enough to make a killing. When all the ships had arrived, the convoy set off for Britain. This convoy was typical of many which braved the dangers of the North Atlantic during 1939–45.

Bill, one of the sailors who travelled with that convoy, will tell us what it was like:

'It is bad enough having to cross the North Atlantic at all. Your ship pitches and rolls as great green seas come crashing over her. Not many ship owners bother about making their crews comfortable or care about giving them decent food. Sailing in a convoy made things worse. We all had to lumber along at the pace of the slowest ship in the convoy, perhaps no more than eight or ten knots. Even so, we did not like being close to other vessels. A ship can't be driven like a car, you know. She doesn't have any brakes. If there was an attack, we had to zig-zag to confuse the submarines. We all had to do it the same way, or the whole convoy would have been bumping into each other like children rushing around in a school playground.'

'What happened during an attack?' 'The first thing you heard was a bang as some unlucky ship was hit. I remember a submarine coming right up into the

the corvette *HMS Hadleigh Castle*

middle of that convoy. She torpedoed a tanker carrying petrol, so there was a great explosion. The sea itself was a mass of flames, and all the crew were killed. Our alarm bells rang and we went to our action stations. I was a wireless operator, so I went to my cabin. The really unlucky ones were the engineers. They had to go to the engine room which was low down in the middle of the ship, just where the submarines aimed their torpedoes. As the corvettes rushed to find the U-boat, we heard the "crump" of depth charges, and huge fountains of water shot into the air. The U-boats attacked us on four days in a row. Our ship was hit on the last day and we had to take to our life-boats. We spent some very uncomfortable hours until one of the escort vessels picked us up. I still have a bad ear because of that day in the sea. We were lucky though, as most of our convoy managed to reach Britain safely.'

'*How many times were you torpedoed altogether?*' 'Three times, which was very unlucky. Some sailors crossed the Atlantic many times throughout the War and never even heard a depth charge explode. I stopped feeling sorry for myself, though, when I heard of a lad of seventeen who was torpedoed six times as well as being taken prisoner by the German battleship *Graf Spee*.

'*Could the merchant ships fight back?*' 'We couldn't fight back against submarines, but we did our best against aircraft. The Germans used to send out big Focke-Wulf Condors to work with the U-boats. We had our machine guns and pom-pom guns to fire at them. Some ships were "catapult aircraft merchantmen". They could catapult a fighter plane into the air. There was nowhere for it to land, of course, so when he had used all his petrol, the pilot came down by parachute and the plane crashed in the sea. We also had some strange devices for shooting wires up into the air. I never heard of any enemy aircraft being damaged that way, but I have known sailors lose a leg or a hand as the wire flew up.'

'*How do you feel about the War now that it's over?*' 'It's strange, but I mainly remember the good things and the funny ones, like the way we had our own back on a captain we hated. We taught his parrot to swear at him. The War left its mark though. Sometimes I have nightmares. Two torpedoes are chasing me and however I twist and turn they follow me. There is no escape. It may seem a silly dream to you, but when I have it I wake up so frightened that I cannot get to sleep again. There must be hundreds of people like me.'

Convoy

a painting by N. Wilkinson of a convoy under attack

a painting by F. Dob

Everythir
fighting
kind of th

'Joh
his hom
bombed
were to
anxiously
had been
After he
mother s
been asl
terrible e
house ne
own hou
father m
country.
and worl
She was
settle. Sl
and afte
stayed tl
so much
was alw
and to k

'Joh
War wa
missed
so differe
get used

evacuees

the Second World
went on working
houses to be built
redecorating old h
formed he joined t
weekends training
that they could
Germans invaded.
had not been calle
or became Air Rai
'The War cam
started to bomb E
cities. When the
and listened for
usually came, foll
a red glow in the
and had too little
but if it happened
an Anderson shelt
quite often half-f
first few times th
remember the dar
of being woken u
taken into the gar

Norman Wilkinson

The H...

Work Section

which stood
various larg
closed beca
generous w
and nylon s
children wo
chase after
Street. The
because ma
black person
too, and we
food whene

'My mo
the War. At
concentrate
allowed us
sugar, etc.,
goods the
ration book
money and
to plan th
became dif
number of
very few n
their old cl
called "Ma
worried my
on bread in
well during
because w
vegetables
fish, werei
Whenever
for fish an
mother fou
took a gre
much was
of a splen
window ar
mouths wa
were ratio
coupons yo
A shopkee
mirror tha
wanted un

W
Se
He
ye

fu
fo
to
fe
so
in
be
ta
G
be
jo
w
h
d
fi

h
W
W
b
a
q
t
u

g

Understand Your Work

1 Dreadnought
1 Why did the Royal Navy seem very powerful in 1897?
2 What was wrong with some of the ships of the Royal Navy?
3 Why were the sailors uncomfortable?
4 What modern methods of fighting were the Navy neglecting?
5 How did Admiral Fisher improve life for the sailors?
6 What college did he start? Why?
7 How long did Fisher's new ship take to build?
8 How many twelve-inch guns did the *Dreadnought* carry? How did that compare with other ships?
9 Why was the *Dreadnought* fast, in spite of her size?
10 How did Sir John Fisher think the *Dreadnought* would deal with an enemy ship in a battle?

2 The Battle of Jutland
1 What did the Germans do after the British built the *Dreadnought*?
2 Where was the British fleet at the beginning of the War? Why?
3 Why did Admiral Jellicoe need to be very careful?
4 Why did the Germans want to avoid a battle?
5 Why was Admiral Scheer compelled to fight at Jutland?
6 In what ways did the German navy prove better than the British?
7 Where did the British and German fleets go after the battle?
8 How did the German U-boats come near to defeating Britain?
9 How were the U-boats defeated in the end?
10 What happened to the German navy after the War?

3 Life in the Trenches
1 Why was it easy for soldiers and their families to keep in touch with each other?
2 Why was neither army able to advance?
3 Why did soldiers dig trenches?
4 How many miles of trenches were there altogether?
5 What made life in the trenches uncomfortable?
6 What food did the soldiers have?
7 What worried them most?
8 What did the soldiers have to do before dawn? Why?
9 How did they spend the day?
10 What work did they do at night?

4 The First Tanks
1 Who first thought of building tanks?
2 What gave him the idea?
3 Why were the first tanks developed by the navy?
4 How did the tank get its name?
5 What was the difference between 'male' and 'female' tanks?
6 Why is it unpleasant to be in a tank?
7 What battle did tanks win in 1917?

8 What German defences did they overrun?
9 How did they cross anti-tank ditches?
10 Why did the British fail to follow up their victory?

5 The Battle of Britain
1 Why was the German army unable to cross the English channel?
2 What event, earlier in the War, made Goering think Britain could be conquered from the air?
3 What would protect the German bombers from the British fighter planes?
4 What warned the British that the German aeroplanes were coming?
5 What weapons did the Messerschmitt and the Spitfire carry?
6 When was the Messerschmitt better than the Spitfire?
7 Why were the German pilots better than most of the British pilots?
8 Why did Sir Hugh Dowding send only a few of his fighters into battle at a time?
9 What important work did Lord Beaverbrook do?
10 What mistake did Hitler and Goering make?

6 War in the Desert
1 Why did the British Eighth Army fight to defend the Western Desert?
2 Why did the British defeat the Italians?
3 Which German general drove the British back?
4 What was unpleasant about fighting in the desert?
5 What was wrong with the Crusader tank?
6 What did its crew fear most?
7 What new weapons did Rommel use?
8 What tanks did the Americans send?
9 Which general took charge of the Eighth Army?
10 Which battle did he win?

7 Convoy
1 How did the defeat of France help the German U-boats?
2 What name was given to a group of U-boats?
3 Why did the British start convoys as soon as the Second World War began?
4 Who took charge of the merchant ships in a convoy?
5 What ships escorted the convoys?
6 Where did they place themselves?
7 Why was it difficult for merchant ships to sail in convoy?
8 How did the escort vessels attack the submarines?
9 How could a merchant ship defend herself?
10 In what ways is Bill still suffering from the War?

8 The Home Front
1 What training did some school boys have during the War?
2 What did Air Raid Wardens teach school children?
3 Why were many women and children evacuated from

London?

4 Why did some of them return to the city?
5 What foreign troops came to Britain during the War?
6 How did the Government make sure everyone had a fair share of food?
7 What was 'Make do and mend'? Why was it necessary?
8 Why did housewives often have to queue?
9 What was the 'Black market'?
10 What organizations did the men who were left at home join?
11 What did some families have for protection during air raids?
12 In what ways was the Second World War less terrible for Britain than the First?

12 Write down the orders for a convoy made by a) the Senior Naval Officer; b) the Commodore. (7)
13 You are a German sailor in a U-boat that is attacking a convoy. Give a running commentary on what happens. (7)
14 You have been evacuated from London during the War. Write a letter to your parents asking them to let you come back home, telling them what it is you do not like in the country. (8)
15 You are a housewife, bringing up a family during the War. Explain what problems and worries you have. (8)

Use Your Imagination

1 You are an admiral in the Royal Navy in 1897. Write a report on the Navy to send to the Government. (1)
2 It is 1906. You are a German admiral and you have just heard about H.M.S. *Dreadnought*. Write a letter to the German Government saying what you think it should do. (1, 2)
3 Give the running commentary that 'Mr. Johnston' might have made on the Battle of Jutland. (2)
4 A British sailor and a German sailor meet after the War. Each claims his own side won the Battle of Jutland and they have an argument. Write what they say. (2)
5 Write a story about a soldier who fought in the trenches during the First World War. (3)
6 You are Colonel Ernest Swinton. It is 1914. Write a letter to the Commander in Chief trying to persuade him that the British Army should have tanks. (4)
7 You are a German who fought at the Battle of Cambrai. Write a letter home telling your parents what happened. (4)
8 Hermann Goering gives his plans for the conquest of Britain and explains why he is sure they will succeed. Write what he says. (5)
9 What do you think would have happened if the German air force had won the Battle of Britain? (5)
10 It is the summer of 1942, several months before the Battle of El Alamein. You are a newspaper reporter in the Western Desert. Send an account of the fighting to your newspaper, explaining why the British Eighth Army is being defeated. (6)
11 Write some extracts from a diary a German soldier might have kept while he was fighting in North Africa. (6)

Further Work

1 Find out what naval battles were fought during the First World War, apart from Jutland.
2 Read descriptions of some of the big battles fought in France during the First World War, e.g. the Marne, the Somme, Verdun and Passchendaele.
3 Find out why the British attacked the Dardanelles, and why they failed.
4 In the First World War the Russians fought against the Germans as allies of the British and French. Read about the war on the Eastern Front.
5 Find out why the Germans were so successful at the beginning of the Second World War. It will help you to understand this if you look at the way they organized their Panzer Divisions.
6 Read about the fighting between Germany and Russia in the Second World War.
7 Find out what you can about the fighting against Japan during the Second World War.
8 Read about the war at sea during the Second World War, especially the ways in which the U-boats were defeated.
9 Find out which of your local buildings are replacements of others destroyed during the Second World War. Are there any other reminders of the War in your area, e.g. pill boxes or an old airfield?
10 Collect pictures of weapons, tanks, ships and aircraft of the two World Wars. Mount them in a scrap book, in a sensible order, and write a description of each one.

The Publisher would like to thank the following for
permission to reproduce photographs:

Austin Morris, Longbridge, p.10; Barnaby's Picture Library, p.75
(bottom); Dr. Barnardo's, p.84; Chris Bonington, p.24 (top);
John Brennan, p.50 and p.124 (top); Bristol City Art Gallery,
p.125; Bruce Coleman Limited, p.24 (bottom) and p.25
(bottom); Cooper–Bridgeman Library, p.105; Cunard Leisure,
p.5; Department of the Environment, Slide Library, p.86;
J. K. Ellwood, p.73; Mary Evans Picture Library, p.54 and p.89;
Nick Fogden, p.97; Foster Associates, p.45; IBM, United
Kingdom, p.45; Imperial War Museum, pp.104–5, p.107,
p.108, p.111, p.113, pp.114–5, p.119 and pp.120–1;
Raymond Irons, p.36 and p.37; John Johnson Collection, p.109;
London Art Technical Drawings Limited, p.11; Mansell
Collection, p.16; Jonathan Martin, p.101; Massey-Ferguson,
p.83; Museum of London, p.88; National Film Archive Stills
Library, p.61; National Motor Museum, Beaulieu (Courtesy of
Robert Hardin Associates), p.8 and p.9; Northern Engineering
Industries Limited, p.4; Popperfoto, p.20, p.21 (bottom), p.22,
p.23 (bottom), p.68, p.109 (bottom) and p.122; Eliot Porter,
p.22 and p.23; Radio Times Hulton Picture Library, p.5, p.14,
p.15, p.17, p.26 (bottom), p.33, p.34, p.35, p.49, p.52, p.60,
p.71, p.78, p.85, p.86 (left), p.88 (bottom), p.92, p.96, p.100,
p.113 (right), p.117, p.122 (bottom) and p.124; Ann Ronan
Picture Library, p.53; Royal Geographical Society, p.21, p.25
(bottom), p.26 (top) and p.27; Science Museum, p.112; Peter
Speed, p.30; John Topham Picture Library, p.69, p.73 (top
right and bottom), p.75 (top) and p.79; U.S. Navy, p.23 (top).

Illustrations by Victor Ambrus, Robert Ayton, Norma Burgin,
Jeff Burn, Stephen Cocking, Chris Fawcey, Terry Hadler, Tom
McArthur, Christine Molan, Tony Morris, John Nash, Paul
Nash, Leonard Rosoman, Graham Smith, Robert H. Smith,
Michael Whittlesea, N. Wilkinson and Maurice Wilson.

The cover illustration, by Christine Molan, shows two children
awaiting evacuation from London to the country at the
beginning of the Second World War.